What people are :
Navigating Life s ivuze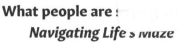

Steve has provided for each Christian a concise roadmap for handling life. The content of this work contains practical teaching on how to walk the "maze" of life which God has intended for us. Each chapter contains crisp biblical content, practical instruction and pithy stories to illustrate the principles he teaches. Further, his personal review and challenge section at the end of these chapters make the reader engage with the content, not just having participated in an intellectual experience. Whatever your place in your Christian walk, you will profit from the biblical insights of this book.

K. Keith Megilligan, D.Min.
Retired Pastor | Bible Professor

If you are searching for the path God has for you, *Navigating Life's Maze* is the book for you! Steve expertly guides you on a journey through the twists and turns of the life of Abram and challenges you with thought-provoking questions and soul-searching practical principles to use on your own road with Jesus.

Phillip Hogan
Youth Minister | Meeker First Baptist Church

My friend and encourager, Steve Baird, writes with depth, purpose, and wit as he offers practical application for Christ-followers in his latest book *Navigating Life's Maze*. Using the example of the Patriarch of our faith, Steve presents a useful life manual for those interested in deepening their walk with the Lord. Sprinkled with quotes and well-seasoned with Scripture, *Navigating Life's Maze* gives readers the essential tools needed to navigate through the challenges, twists, and turns of life.

John B. Brittain, PhD
Associational Mission Strategist | West Central Baptist Association

NAVIGATING LIFE'S MAZE

Following Abraham's Footsteps to the Will of God

STEVE BAIRD

Navigating Life's Maze
Copyright 2020 by Steven Baird

ISBN: 978-1-7323979-4-1 (paperback)
ISBN: 978-1-7323979-5-8 (e-book)
ISBN: 978-1-7323979-6-5 (hardcover)
Library of Congress Control Number: 2020910750

Contact Steve Baird at e710ministries@gmail.com or www.e710ministries.com

Gold foil cover artwork by http://graphicflip.com
Editing and Proofreading: Jennifer Harshman, HarshmanServices.com
Book Design and Production: James Woosley, FreeAgentPress.com

DEDICATION

*This book is dedicated to my Mom and Dad,
Dorrell and Lindy Baird.*

*I am thankful you encouraged me
as I navigated life's maze.*

*I am grateful you continually asked me
what God's will for my life was and
encouraged me to faithfully follow it.*

CONTENTS

PREFACE

How to Use
Navigating Life's Maze

NAVIGATING LIFE'S MAZE CAN BE used in many different ways. It is designed to be read and used individually or in a group. Below briefly outlines those usages.

First, one can read the book and process the material for him or herself.

Second, one can read the book and work though the study guide that follows each chapter.

Third, a small group can read the book and process the material as they would like.

Fourth, a small group can meet to discuss the chapters and use the study guide as a help for processing each chapter. There are two ways the group can precede. 1) The group can meet and introduce the book to become familiar with the material. Then over the next week, they can read the chapter, and answer the study guide questions to discuss at the next small group meeting. 2) Before the first meeting, the group can read the chapter, work through the study guide on their own, and come prepared to discussion the material.

Whatever way you chose to use *Navigating Life's Maze*, God is waiting for you just inside the doorway to direct you through life's maze.

INTRODUCTION

THE
FIRST
STEP

INTO THE MAZE OF HAY BALES

EACH YEAR THE SAME OPPONENTS wage the same war, at the same time, and the outcome is always the same. One contestant is summer. Summer's battle plan is to grip us with its infamous fingers of heat and humidity. As one month of summer melts into the next, the calendar alerts us to the coming clash. The other contestant is autumn. Autumn's battle plan is to douse us with its infamous breath of cold rains and frosty mornings. But before the struggle is over and autumn emerges as victor, there is an amazing period when these diverse seasons seemingly work together. God's unparalleled creativity briefly opens a window to allow the breeze of pleasant days and cool nights to sweep into our lives. During these unique days, an interesting phenomenon occurs. We find a welcome break from the hottest summer ever since the last one, and we experience selective memory lost as last year's dampest autumn pales in comparison to this one. It is during this sliver of time that we may find ourselves making a trip to the pumpkin patch, eating s'mores around a cozy fire, sipping on hot chocolate, snuggling in our favorite blankie, feeding farm animals, taking a hayride, or navigating our way through a maze.

When our three boys were little, my wife would orchestrate a wonderful plan each year for a family outing to enjoy this changing of the guard. I would look forward to this time of picking out pumpkins, feeding farm animals, going on a hayride, sliding down the slide as much as the boys did. Suddenly, my wife would have four boys to keep an eye on and out of trouble at the farms. Notice, my list of anticipated things to do did not include the maze. I am not particularly fond of mazes, but I think I have a good reason – at least that's my story and I'm sticking to it!

My oldest son, Noah, was about four years old when we went to an incredible, amazing, mind-boggling, scary, anxiety-filled, one-of-a-kind maze. I think I included all the adjectives that are important to describing this maze. It was made of bales of hay which were stacked about four or five bales high and laid out in a rectangular shape. The maze itself was completely enclosed with bales of hay on top, on bottom, and on all the sides. It had one opening in the front and one in the rear, both about the size of two bales of hay. When we entered the maze, my son could stand up in it, but, as an adult, I had to crawl on my hands and knees on the hay bale floor.

Once we made it past the first corner, we were engulfed by a tidal wave of blackness. This absence of light was so thick I could feel the darkness pressing against me creating confusion and disorientation. As we slowly inched along, the hay bales beneath me, beside me, and above me created hay dust that made it difficult to breathe and fully awakened my claustrophobia. Though I could not see it in the dark, I think I turned a shade of green from the anxiety; however, I know I did feel the strong urges of the Incredible Hulk to break through the walls of my hay bale prison. I needed freedom. Then it hit me. I could not freak out and break through the maze, I needed to be the "cool" Dad. Somehow, we maneuvered around the next corner and there... there was a child with a LIGHT! I wanted to adopt him on the spot! However, the "cool" Dad prevailed. I suggested that we all stay together and help each other through this darkness that had a grip on us (or should I say me).

With the assistance of my new best friend and his amazing light of comfort, my son and I made it through the hay bale maze to see the sunlight, breathe fresh air, and walk on Terra Firma again. The relief I experienced quickly turned to panic as I glanced at my son. He had that wide-eyed look of excitement and wonder that only a four-year-old could have. "Let's do it again!" he exclaimed with glee. Usually my heart would have leapt into my throat, but this time it by-passed my throat and went straight to my mind: *"How could I do this again?"* *"Maybe my wife would like to go, and I could stay with our other son?"* *"Where was my 'adopted child' with the light?"* But then my image to be the "cool" Dad gave way to my desire to be the "caring" Dad: *"How could I not do this again with my son?"* So, off we went for round two.

Shortly after entering the maze of terror, I gained a little better understanding of God's grace. I did not deserve this gift from God, but there...

there was another child with a LIGHT! Thinking a bit more rationally, I did not want to adopt this child, but only to "borrow" the child and his light to speedily make it through the maze. After exiting the maze for a painstaking second time, I was just beginning to get my sea legs, or in this case land legs, when I heard that four-year-old voice proclaim: *"Again!"* At this point, I reached into my parenting toolbox and grabbed one of the two tools I had acquired as a young parent. It was the great parenting technique of distraction. *"Oh, there are many other things to see and do here at the pumpkin patch,"* I stated as I directed his attention away from the maze. During the remainder of our time at the farm, I avoided the area of the maze like it was poison ivy and never mentioned it as if it was a bad word. Fortunately, it came time to leave for home without any more *"incidents"* in the maze. Now in his twenties, my son has no memory of his maze of fun, but I carry an emotional scar from this maze of fright.

We are about to take the first step into another maze. A maze of excitement and a maze of terror. It is the maze we call life.

With every step you take,
think about what he wants,
and he will help you go the right way.
Proverbs 3:6 (ERV)

INTO THE MAZE OF LIFE

Another kind of war invades our lives. Though the opponents are the same, the time, the place, and the outcome often vary. The battle is between our will and God's will. Sometimes, the skirmish is subtle. Other times, the conflict rages. And at times, the struggle is not between our will and God's but rather what is God's will.

The changing of the seasons in our lives often brings a clash of wills as we decide about where to go to college, who to marry, which career to pursue, where to move, when to retire, or why to follow Jesus. During the seasons of our lives, we come face to face with the showdown of wills as we purchase a home, change a career, decide on a church, and start a family or a business. We engage in countless wrestling matches that are advertised on the marquee as "Our Will" vs. "God's Will." Decisions are made about confronting a co-worker, disciplining our child, buying a car, or choosing a course of medical treatment. Are the seemingly small matters in life, like deciding on a brand of toothpaste, choosing a route to drive to my destination, or picking a color to paint my bedroom, really sneak attacks that put my will and God's will at odds?

Suddenly we experience the "maze of hay bales" and all its challenges, but this time it is labeled the "maze of life." As we pursue the living God throughout the maze of our lives, these "major battles," "medium battles," "minor battles," and "minuscule battles" have significance. Each of us is currently in a battle that should drive us to pray, "O most merciful redeemer, friend and brother, may I know thee more clearly, love thee more dearly and follow thee more nearly, day by day."[1]

> The key is not to have a large amount of faith in a small God, but a small amount of faith in a large God.
> **MARK EDWARDS, MISSIONARY**

Many parallels emerge between my experience in the maze of hay bales and our journey through the maze of life. The maze I experienced was much darker than imagined, and many times life is very dark. As the child with the light provided comfort and help along the path, God may place someone just around the next corner to go with us and carry the light of God's Word. God graciously provides us with just enough light for our next step through His Word, which is a lamp to our feet and a light for our path.[2]

As I proceeded slowly through the maze, I was overtaken by two bullies: confusion and disorientation. At times we don't know if we should go to the right or the left. This is when we must not allow confusion, disorientation, and their henchmen fear and indecision keep us from clearly hearing Jesus' voice calling to us: *"Come to me, all you who are weary and burdened, and I will give you rest"* (Matthew 11:28).

In my mind, the walls of the hay bale maze crept in closer and closer and closer. On occasions life seems to narrow, and the walls press in on every side of us. When we feel as though our very life is being squeezed from us, recognize that others have followed Jesus through this very same narrow spot in the maze. The Apostle Paul vividly depicts the troubles, despair, and struggles we will encounter along the way. No matter how difficult his time in life's maze was, Paul wanted others to see Jesus in him. Notice God's will for all of us as we navigate life's maze.

> We now have this light shining in our hearts, but we ourselves are like fragile clay jars containing this great treasure. This makes it clear that our great power is from God, not from ourselves. We are pressed on every side by troubles, but we are not crushed. We are perplexed, but not driven to despair. We are hunted down, but never abandoned by God. We get knocked down, but we are not destroyed. Through suffering, our bodies continue to share in the death of Jesus **so that the life of Jesus may also be seen in our bodies**. (2 Corinthians 4:7–10 NLT)

We would be remiss to not zero in on a couple of observations from my son's experience in the maze. He exhibited excitement, joy, and intrigue as we made our way through the hay bale maze. Following Jesus Christ is an adventure. He demonstrated a complete calm and peace as he looked to me to lead him through the maze. When we actively concentrate our focus on Jesus, we are assured of His presence, His peace, and His guidance in midst of the maze, because Jesus is "the author, pioneer, and finisher of our faith"[3] and the maze of life.

Whether it is a relationship, circumstance, issue, decision, or a multitude of other life matters, pursuing God's will for our lives can feel like we are navigating our way through a maze. It can be an exhilarating adventure and a frustrating endeavor. At times, it may seem as though we take three steps forward and two steps backward. But be encouraged, God has not brought us this far to leave us now. He leads us to a wall in the maze in order to face areas we have not yet given to Him. God allows us to follow a path to a dead end in order to capture our attention, hearts, and wills. In this maze of life we will find a friend who will remind us that in the Christian life, victory comes through surrender!

INTO THE MAZE OF A FRIEND

The battle of our wills is a war that continually creeps into our lives to bring us face-to-face with our own pride, neglect, and stubbornness. The victory that comes through the Lord begins to emerge and is evident in the lives of others like Abraham, *"Now these things happened to them (those in the Old Testament, including Abraham) as an example, but they were written down for our instruction, on whom the end of the ages has come"* 1 Corinthians 10:11 (ESV). We find we are not alone in the battle. As we closely examine the lives of these men and women of the Scriptures, they serve as an example for us. Their stories have been recorded to allow them to be our guides, companions, and friends in the maze.

We want to take time to become close friends with Abraham because he invites us to maneuver through the maze of life with him, to learn from the steps he took, to be individuals of faith, and ultimately to be called God's friend. Along the way, Abraham gives us five steps to navigate our way to the will of God in the maze of life. Each step is a principle that acts as a compass in the maze. We carefully pack in our knapsack this needed supply of principles and allow Abraham to help us pull them out at just right moment.

As we put these compasses in our knapsack for the journey ahead of us, let us briefly become acquainted with each principle. For each principle is a compass to guide us to take the next step in our walk with Jesus.

➤ **The Step of Willingness:**
Be willing to do whatever God wants. Abraham was willing to leave everything to follow God, even when he did not know where God was leading him. The road to God's will always will go through a heart of willingness to do whatever God desires.

➤ **The Step of Obedience:**
Be obedient to what you know God wants. Abraham was obedient to what God asked him. Though he was not without sin, in faith Abraham did some very difficult things that God asked him to do. Our Step of Obedience demonstrates our love for the Lord.

➤ **The Step of Wholeheartedness:**
Be wholehearted in giving yourself to what God wants. Throughout his life, Abraham gave the Lord more and more of his heart until God had it all. It will be a lifelong struggle between wholeheartedness and half-heartedness in our journey with the Lord. God is continually at work in our lives to purify us and have more and more of our hearts.

➤ **The Step of Alertness:**
Be looking for what God is doing in your life. Abraham continually looked for the Lord's direction and leading in his life. Abraham often communed with God to focus and refocus on God's will for his life. In the midst of the twists and turns of the maze, it is vital that we stay connected with the Lord and be alert to His leading.

➤ **The Step of Faithfulness:**
Be faithful to what God wants in your life. Abraham had his doubts, wrong allegiances, and sins, but overall, his life was characterized by his faithfulness to his God. His faith was clearly evident, and Abraham was called a friend of God. God values faithfulness and longs for us to "keep on keeping on."

Though each principle is intricately intertwined with the other four, the response of our heart and the need of the situation dictate which principle is to be employed. They are not necessarily sequential, one step building on the previous. They are not to be seen as magical, as though the five steps are some hidden keys to God's will. They may not be revolutionary, but there is a critical need for our eyes to take a fresh look at each principle and take the appropriate first step into God's maze.

INTO THE MAZE OF GOD

Just before we take that first step into God's maze, we discover He has placed something very important in each of our knapsacks. God has given us three nutritional snacks that will serve as foundational truths to hold onto in the maze and to ponder before we commence our adventure.

First, God wants us to know His will. We may experience times in the maze when we feel like God is hiding the next step from us. We might even feel as though God has abandoned us or does not exist, and we are destined to navigate the maze on our own. Though there are times of uncertainty, struggle, and loneliness, God wants us to know, do, and move towards His will more than we do. Take note of Psalm 138:8 (ISV): *"The Lord will complete what his purpose is for me. Lord, your gracious love is eternal; do not abandon your personal work in me."*

Second, God uses everything in our lives, the good, the bad, and the ugly, to develop us and move us towards Him. Some of us may have picked up the notation that God only uses nearly perfect or "super" spiritual individuals. Keep in mind that "God uses people who fail – cause there aren't any other kind around."[4] Walking closely with Abraham will reveal that he is just like us. We will see that God used Abraham whose natural default in times of difficulty was to lie. And God uses us in spite of when we get off track, when we stay on track, when we make mistakes, when we make good decisions, when we commit sin, and when we act like Jesus. God delights in turning our weaknesses into His strength, and He gives us reassurance in His Field Manual:

Each time he [Jesus] said, "My grace is all you need. My power works best in weakness." So now I am glad to boast about my weaknesses, so that the power of Christ can work through me. That's why I take pleasure in my weaknesses, and in the insults, hardships, persecutions, and troubles that I suffer for Christ. For when I am weak, then I am strong. (2 Corinthians 12:9–10 NLT)

Third, God desires that we walk by faith, not sight. We want God to send us a text or a letter or give us a phone call to let us know which path to take but He doesn't work that way. Just like Abraham, our faith is credited to us as righteousness[5] and we please God by living a life of faith.[6] By taking a step of faith, God will reveal the next step of faith and the next and the next until our lives are characterized by what the Apostle Paul said, *"We live by faith, not by sight"* (2 Corinthians 5:7).

So, the time has come to grab your knapsack, a bottle of water, a handful of trail mix, and tighten your sandals. It is time for us to hit the dusty and messy road of life alongside Abraham because:

Abraham's story is our story. In our own way, each of us is a nomad. Like this great man of faith, we have been called to embark on a great spiritual journey toward a destination God will show us (see Genesis 12:1). Abraham's epitaph can also be ours if, like him, we choose to be "fully convinced that God is able to do whatever he promises." Then, like our father in faith, we will be declared righteous on the basis of our trust in Him.[7]

Lord, make me willing to be willing.

Just around the first corner Abraham is waiting enthusiastically for us to join him in the maze. He cannot wait to introduce us to the one, true, living LORD who calls him friend. He is eager to show us how to live a life of faith which is credited to us as righteousness. Abraham will not hold back as he candidly shares with us the sins, wrong turns, and regrets he made. Abraham invites us to take the next step which is the

Step of Willingness. This step will demonstrate to us that at times we willingly follow the Lord, and at other times we must pray, *"Lord, make me willing to be willing!"* Willingness may be the easiest, hardest step we take. With that in mind, let's join Abraham in navigating this maze we call life.

MY FIRST STEP

THE FIRST STEP INTO THE MAZE

➤ How does the author's story about the hay bale maze help you relate to the maze of life?

➤ How is Proverbs 3:6 a challenge to you as you look into your life's maze?

With every step you take, think about what he wants, and he will help you go the right way.
—PROVERBS 3:6 (ERV)

THE FIRST STEP INTO THE BATTLE

➤ How is following God's will for you like a battle?

➤ In the battle of the maze, what did Jesus mean when He said, *"Come to me, all you who are weary and burdened, and I will give you rest"* (Matthew 11:28)?

➤ Why is it important in the battle of the Christian life to remember, *"Victory comes through surrender?"*

THE FIRST STEP WITH A FRIEND

➢ Why is it important to allow Abraham to become our friend? How will you become his friend in the maze?

➤ Of the five principles that we will carry in our knapsack while we are in the maze of life:

1. The Step of Willingness
2. The Step of Obedience
3. The Step of Wholeheartedness
4. The Step of Alertness
5. The Step of Faithfulness

- Which one are you looking forward to learning more about? Why?

- Which one are you not so interested in? Why?

THE FIRST STEP WITH THE LORD

Of the three foundational truths discussed:

Put a ☆ by the one(s) that is the most encouraging to you right now.

Put a ○ by the one(s) that is the most disconcerting to you right now.

Put a ✡ by the one(s) that is the hardest to believe for you right now.

Put a ✝ by the one(s) that is the most needed by you right now.

1. God wants us to know His will.

2. God uses everything in our lives.

3. God desires that we walk by faith, not sight.

➤ As you grab your knapsack, a bottle of water, a handful of trail mix, and tighten your sandals, take the challenge you wrote earlier from Proverbs 3:6 and now write it as a prayer to the LORD.

Listen to me, all who hope for deliverance—
all who seek the Lord!
Consider the rock from which you were cut,
the quarry from which you were mined.
Yes, think about Abraham, your ancestor,
and Sarah, who gave birth to your nation.
Abraham was only one man when I called him.
But when I blessed him, he became a great nation.

ISAIAH 51:1–2 (NLT)

CHAPTER 1

THE VOLUNTOLD STEP

AN UNFAMILIAR WORD FOR THE MAZE

FOR OVER FIVE DECADES, IT was not a word in my vocabulary; in fact, I don't even recall hearing it. This interesting new-to-me word is tossed around my workplace like a football. At times, individuals catch this football in stride scoring touchdowns, and other times it bonks them in the nose, ala Marcia Brady. I thought a quick look in the dictionary would prove that the word had been made up. My investigation into the dictionary revealed that "voluntold" was an

actual word being defined as: *"The exact opposite of volunteering. Always used in reference to an unpleasant task to which you have been assigned by your boss."*[1] The dictionary definition was a bit different than my perception of the word and its usage among my co-workers. So, I perused the bookshelves of my mind until I found that often used fictionist book:

Baird's Attempt to Define Everyday Words or **BADEW**[2] for short. I pulled it off the shelf, opened to the appropriate page, and discovered a slight variation in my mind's understanding. "Voluntold [vol-uhn-tohld] forms a meaning that comes from the combination of two words: 'volunteer', where someone offers their services or takes on an undertaking and 'told', where an individual is assigned a particular duty without volunteering." This middle ground of the tension between volunteering and being told is where we will start with the word "voluntold."

Without an invitation, voluntold sneaks through just the slightest of cracks in our thinking. This intrusion suddenly creates a discomfort that might equate to the prickly feeling of a caterpillar creeping down the back of our neck and into our shirt. Jesus could not have been clearer when He invites us to *"Come, follow Me"* (Matthew 4:19; John 1:43). But at the same time, Jesus could not have stated it more plainly when He said, *"Whoever wants to be my disciple must deny themselves and take up their cross daily and follow me"* (Luke 9:23). Deep within our hearts and minds is a pull in which we find ourselves wanting to follow Jesus willingly, but at the same time feeling "told" to follow Jesus. It is at this point that we might feel the call to follow Jesus is a bit like being "voluntold."

As we enter the maze of life to walk with Abram[3], the very first turn brings us face-to-face with the struggle of feeling voluntold. Perhaps we did not anticipate encountering this, at least not yet. It is the mysterious battle of the will and motives. We do not like to visit this murky corner of our hearts, because the prophet Jeremiah's luminous words chase away the darkness to expose the distasteful description of each of our heart's natural inclination: *"The human heart is the most deceitful of all things, and desperately wicked. Who really knows how bad it is?"* (Jeremiah 17:9 NLT). However, we want to also examine the spiritual heart given to us in Christ Jesus. The Apostle Paul shines light on this new heart in Christ: *"And those who belong to Christ Jesus have crucified the flesh with its passions and desires. If we live by the Spirit, let us also keep in step with the Spirit"* (Galatians 5:24–25 ESV). Our natural desires and our spiritual desires are like the ends of a magnet that repel each other. *"For the desires of the flesh are against the Spirit, and the desires of the Spirit are against the flesh, for these are opposed to each other, to keep you from doing the things you want to do"* (Galatians 5:17 ESV).[4] Perhaps we hoped to ease into the war, but as we run up against this first wall in the maze, we are thrust into the fury of the battle at the front lines. We are now fully engaged in hand to hand combat with our wills and our motives.

Our own motives are tricky and hard to determine at best. Our own wills are stubborn and typically won't surrender without a vicious brawl. If I wait until I am fully willing to follow Jesus, I may never follow Him, but if I follow Jesus because I am commanded or expected, then I may not be following Jesus from a heart of love. What a conundrum! It does feel a bit like being voluntold, and this is where we join Abram. We join him to take the Step of Willingness, a willingness that navigates us down the path in the maze wherever the Lord wants us to go. As we travel this road, we will need the ear of attention, the heart of abandonment, and the feet of alignment.

LORD, I know that people's lives are not their own; it is not for them to direct their steps.
Jeremiah 10:23

TAKE THE STEP OF WILLINGNESS IN THE MAZE

THE STEP OF WILLINGNESS MEANS WE HAVE AN EAR OF ATTENTION.

> The Lord had said to Abram, "Go from your country, your people, and your father's household to the land I will show you."
> **Genesis 12:1**

To best grasp the understanding of Genesis 12:1, *"The LORD had said to Abram,"* let us pause to examine its backdrop found in the preceding verses, Genesis 11:26–32:

> After Terah had lived 70 years, he became the father of Abram, Nahor and Haran. This is the account of Terah's family line. Terah became the father of Abram, Nahor and Haran. And Haran became the father of Lot. While his father Terah was still alive, Haran died in Ur of the Chaldeans, in the land of his birth. Abram and Nahor both married. The name of Abram's wife was Sarai, and the name of Nahor's wife was Milkah; she was the daughter of Haran, the father of both Milkah and Iskah. Now Sarai was childless because she was not able to conceive. Terah took his son Abram, his grandson Lot son of Haran, and his daughter-in-law Sarai, the wife of his son Abram, and together they set out from Ur of the Chaldeans to go to Canaan. But when they came to Haran, they settled there. Terah lived 205 years, and he died in Harran.

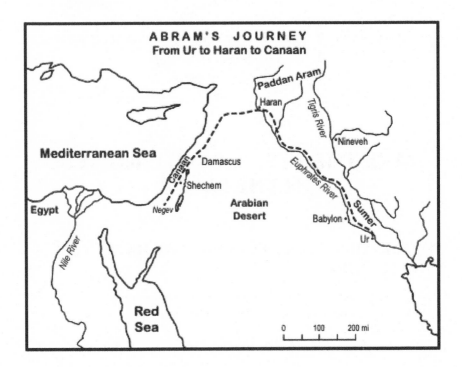

A few observations are in order: 1) Abram was born, lived, and was married in Ur of the Chaldeans; 2) Abram's wife Sarai was barren; 3) Terah, Abram, Sarai, and Lot set out for Canaan; 4) They all settled in Haran; 5) Terah died in Haran.

The Lord's original call to Abram was while he was in Ur of the Chaldeans (Genesis 11:28, 31; Acts 7:4), but for some reason the caravan "settled in Haran." Many questions about this "layover" in Haran might come to mind like: "After 550 miles of travel, did Abram become weary in following God's directions?" "Was Abram sidetracked because of some influence, perhaps Terah?" "Did Abram allow other gods to capture his heart's worship?" "Had something creeped into Abram's life to bog him down from moving forward as the Lord directed?" The complete answers to these questions regarding Abram may leave us puzzled or elude us altogether, but they are an appropriate springboard to ask ourselves: "As I follow Jesus, have I become weary in His call for me?" "Has something or someone influenced me to stop my pursuit of Christ?" "Has something or someone crept into the place in my life that only God deserves?" "Am I trying to carry extra baggage through the maze of life?" Honest answers to these questions may leave us with an uneasy feeling or elude us altogether, but this is right where God wants us to be so we can join Abram in the maze. This is where we begin to encounter the principle of willingness.

> Faith demands a ruthless abandonment of the past.[5]
>
> **BRUCE WALTKE, COMMENTATOR**

"The Lord had said to Abram" (Genesis 12:1) informs us that God's past call to Abram to go to Canaan is now reiterated. As we enter the tenuous step of our wills, it is important that we recognize that many times the Lord is a God of second calls. The river of God's grace creates a deep ravine that runs throughout the Word of God as we see Him offering second chances (or third or even more). Abram, Jeremiah, and our famous friend Jonah experienced a second call to willingly follow God. Interestingly, the Lord's disciples required more than one, "Come and follow Me" moment. The disciples followed Jesus, but then a few chapters later we find them down at the lake fishing again. Jesus comes and repeats His call, "Follow Me." We may have taken a wrong turn in our maze or we may have completely stopped, but be encouraged by our travel companions who did the same thing, and God graciously continued to work with them a second or third or tenth time.

A word of caution is needful. We must listen when God speaks, because we are not guaranteed more than one call. Each time we resist God's voice, it gets softer and softer until it goes unnoticed. Each time we refuse to take a willing step in God's direction or make no decision at all, our hearts become a little colder and a little more callous towards the things of God. Then we may find ourselves in a place we never dreamt, doing something we could not imagine, and being a person we never intended to be.

Willingness is perhaps the hardest step one finds in the maze, and it begins by having an ear of attentiveness to the voice of God. God spoke, and Abram listened. Listening must lead to action. We see Abram's ear of attentiveness led to his leaving Haran for Canaan (Genesis 12:4).

A fellow traveler in the maze is Moses, and we gain valuable insight into what it means for us to "listen to the LORD" from him. The book of Deuteronomy records a speech Moses gives to the nation of Israel. His instructions are to: *"**Listen** closely, Israel, and be careful to obey"* (Deuteronomy 6:3a NLT). The word for "listen" has the idea of *paying attention in order to understand and then to put into practice what is said*. Willingness to listen to God with the intent to do what He says is explained by Moses and modeled by Abram.

> O Lord, grant that I may do Thy will as if it were my will, so that Thou mayest do my will as if it were Thy will.
>
> *AUGUSTINE*

To better grasp how the Step of Willingness and the concept of listening to the LORD work in tandem, let us take note of the story about an old country farmer who went to visit his friend in New York. The friend took this country farmer right into the heart of downtown to see the sights and hear the sounds of New York City. They were immersed in the activity and sounds of a city that never sleeps. As the two friends stood on the street corner, they were lambasted by horns blaring, vendors selling, tires screeching, people yelling, motorcycles zooming, sirens screaming, and taxis, well, acting like taxis. With a slow deliberate movement, the farmer brought his finger to his lips, requesting his friend to be quiet. Then the farmer stated matter of factly, "I hear a cricket chirping." The friend wondered if his farmer friend was beginning to experience some strange effects from the exhaust fumes of the vehicles. As the man quieted himself and listened intently, to his amazement, he too heard the chirping of the cricket. The friend exclaimed, "How did you hear that tiny sound of a cricket chirping in the midst of the loud chaos of the city?" Drawing on his years of experience, the farmer again stated matter of factly, "It all depends on what you are listening for."

In the maze of our life, we are lambasted by children yelling, bosses screaming, bills blaring, weekends zooming, and spouses, well, acting like spouses. What are we listening for? Can we hear God when life gets loud, takes unexpected turns, or we run into a wall in the maze? Once we hear the voice of the Lord, we abandon our will for the desires of our Father.

THE STEP OF WILLINGNESS MEANS WE HAVE A HEART OF ABANDONMENT.

> The Lord had said to Abram, "Go from your country, your people and your father's household to the land I will show you."
>
> **Genesis 12:1**

The Step of Willingness not only asks for an ear of attentiveness to God's Word, but it also demands a heart of abandonment to Him. We are to leave everything and everybody for the sake of our LORD.

As Abram listened to Him, God's first word was **"Go."** The biblical scholar Bruce Waltke depicts what this word would have meant to Abram. "The Hebrew expression (go or leave) is that of **'determinedly disassociating oneself,'** literally **'leave by yourself.'"**[6] This is a significant word of willing abandonment. Each of us must make a conscious decision to leave persons, places, and things to willingly follow after Jesus. God asked for Abram to leave it all—his country, people, father, land—and Jesus asks us for this same disassociation.

> Anyone who loves their father or mother more than me is not worthy of me; anyone who loves their son or daughter more than me is not worthy of me. Whoever does not take up their cross and follow me is not worthy of me. Whoever finds their life will lose it, and whoever loses their life for my sake will find it. (Matthew 10:37–39)

As we delve deeply into this concept of *"determinedly dissociating ourselves,"* we note that God is asking for a willing abandonment to Him alone. Abram was to disassociate himself from his country, his people, and his father's household. He was to replace these with a willing allegiance to the true God only. As a great example of faith, perhaps this allegiance seems like a no-brainer, but just as we have many things that vie for our attention, so did Abram. His struggles were the same as ours and this is why he is such a tremendous encouragement to us in the maze. God wants and deserves His rightful place in our lives, but He will not force Himself on us. Instead God longs and waits for us to take this all-important Step of Willingness.

Traveling through the maze of life with Abram we discover an interesting reason that God asks for a heart of abandonment in Abram's life and ours: idols. Though we might not bow before a piece of wood or stone, we each are tempted to give allegiance in an area in our hearts to something or someone that only God deserves. We have idols, and so did Abram.

Before Abram gave his devotion to the LORD God Almighty, his loyalty was to other gods.[7] "Genesis 11 thus sets the stage for the appearance of Abram, whose ancestry locates him in northern Syria [Haran] and whose ancestors appear as figures worshiping different deities. Both locale and belief would change with the calling of God and Abram's response in faith."[8] Joshua 24:2 (ESV) further validates this, *"And Joshua said to all the people, 'Thus says the Lord, the God of Israel, "Long ago, your fathers lived beyond the Euphrates, Terah, the father of Abraham and of Nahor; and **they served other gods**."'"* It seems like an astonishing statement about our hero and father of our faith, Abram, but the truth is he was a real human that faced real conflicts of his will and struggles with abandonment to the true living God over false dead idols. Because our weaknesses are the same as Abram's, he becomes a very relatable traveling companion and close friend in the maze.

> Our God meets us at the point of our need.
> **DICK BEMARKT**

To gain further insight into Abram's heart of abandonment, let us look again at the word found in Genesis 12:1 for "go" or "leave" (lek-leka) and examine it more thoroughly. This Hebrew phrase, lek-eka, only occurs in this form two times in all of the Old Testament and therefore links the two passages. The first is here, where God asks Abram to disassociate himself from his country, people, and his father's household. The second is in Genesis 22:2, where God asks Abram to disassociate himself from Isaac and leave him to the LORD. *"Then God said, 'Take your son, your only son, whom you love—Isaac—and go (lek-leka) to the region of Moriah. Sacrifice him there as a burnt offering on a mountain I will show you'"* (Genesis 22:2). These two incredible events are bookends to the many tests that Abram experienced placing God on the throne of his life.

The great preacher and outstanding author A.W. Tozer (1897–1963) gives valuable insight into this concept of abandonment when he writes, "the child (Isaac) became at once the delight and the idol of his

(Abraham's) heart"[9] and that God was saying to Abraham, "It's all right, Abraham. I never intended that you should actually slay the lad. I only wanted to remove him from the temple of your heart that I might reign unchallenged there. I wanted to correct the perversion that existed in your love."[10]

Under the layers of our lives, we all find "idols" scurrying for cover like bugs in the dark when the light is turned on. Peeling back the inner layers of ourselves exposes our favorite idols. Ones we so carefully try to keep hidden in the deep crevices and dark recesses of our heart. As we seek to pry loose our longing for possessions, pleasures, or position, this is where we take the Step of Willingness. This allows Jesus His rightful place in our lives because an idol is anything or anybody in our life that is in the place that only Jesus deserves.

The apostle Paul tells us how to have a heart of abandonment when he states simply, *"turn to God from idols to serve the living and true God"* (1 Thessalonians 1:9). The formula is straightforward for Abram and for us, but the application is a lifelong journey through the difficulties of life's maze. We make an intentional disassociation **from** the "idol" and then decide **to** pursue the character and nature of Jesus Christ. The Apostle John pleads with tenderness as he warns us about the devious nature of our hearts and the sly attraction of idols, *"Dear children, keep away from anything that might take God's place in your hearts"* (1 John 5:21 NLT).

THE STEP OF WILLINGNESS MEANS WE HAVE THE FEET OF ALIGNMENT.

We must not rush to the next step in the maze before we acknowledge an important component associated with the Step of Willingness. Ears that are attentive and hearts that are abandoned will lead our feet to align with the steps of our Lord. Just as the wheels on our car need to be in alignment, so that we do not drift out of our lane, possibly striking another car or finding ourselves in a ditch, we want to move forward in willingness to align our steps with ones our Savior gives us from the Scriptures.

Throughout his lifetime Abram got out of alignment with the LORD. He ended up in the ditch of lies more than once. He created a major clash of nations as he drifted away from God's plan by trying to fulfill God's will through Hagar. But as we reflect on Abraham's life, we see he also aligned his steps with God's instructions when he left his country and family behind, continually worshiped the living God, and offered his son as a sacrifice to God. As we walk in step with Jesus, He wants our feet to be aligned with Him by allowing His Word to turn us **from** our will **to** God's will.

We are to listen to the Lord with the intent of doing what He says. The Apostle Paul reiterates this concept and the importance of listening to the Word of God for direction, *"So faith comes from hearing, and hearing through the word of Christ"* (Romans 10:17 ESV). God's Word is clear about several specific things that are His will, and highlighted below are a few specific examples of God's will for us that are given in His Word.

- Do not conform to the pattern of this world, but be transformed by the renewing of your mind. Then you will be able to test and approve what God's **will** is—his good, pleasing and perfect **will**. (Romans 12:2)

- **For this is God's will:** that you become holy, that you keep away from sexual immorality. (1 Thessalonians 4:3 NET)

- Be thankful in all circumstances, **for this is God's will** for you who belong to Christ Jesus. (1 Thessalonians 5:18 NLT)

- **It is God's** will that your honorable lives should silence those ignorant people who make foolish accusations against you. (1 Peter 2:15 NLT)

- For it is better, **if it is God's will**, to suffer for doing good than for doing evil. (1 Peter 3:17)

We have noted a sampling of clear instructions God has for us to follow in the maze of life. However, the Scriptures do not give us what to do at every specific turn in our life's maze e.g. who to marry, where to go to college, or what car to purchase. This is where we must be willing to allow the principles of God's word to be a light to guide us so at every juncture, we will reach God's destination for us. The psalmist gives us clear and comforting words when he writes, *"Your word is like a lamp for my feet and a light for my path"* (Psalm 119:105 NCV).

> Most people are bothered by those passages of Scripture they do not understand, but I have always noticed that the passages that bother me are those I do understand.[11]
>
> **MARK TWAIN, AUTHOR**

Picture yourself going through a thick forest on a pitch dark, moonless night. It is hard to find your way and perhaps a bit scary; however, there is a path for you to navigate from one side of the deep forest to the other side. To assist you on the winding path you have only a flashlight. Standing uneasily at the edge of the forest, you shine the light down the path, but you cannot see all the way through the forest. The night is as dark as charcoal, the road meanders like the path of a crawling snake, and the light of your flashlight only gives enough illumination to take the next step or two. With each step the light reveals more of the path. At one point you notice a tree has fallen across the path blocking it, and you must either go around it or over it. Later you steer to the left side of the path, because on the right is a large hole that you want to avoid falling into. Finally, you emerge on the other side of the eerie forest and safely arrive at your destination. The directives and principles of God's Word are like this, giving us enough light to take the next step and the next, avoiding pitfalls, until we reach God's destination for us. This resonates with my experience in the hay bale maze. Once my son and I found the child with the light, his light gave us just enough light for the next step and the next until we reached the exit of the maze, much to my delight!

God's Word gives us clear directives and general principles to follow Jesus through the maze of life, but we must continually feed on the written and living Christ. Even though the Scriptures are God's primary way to speak to us and guide us in the maze, we often neglect it. At times our feeding on God's Word is like, *The Story of Augustus Who Would Not Have Any Soup.*[12]

Augustus was a chubby lad;
Fat ruddy cheeks Augustus had;

And everybody saw with joy;
The plump and hearty healthy boy.

He ate and drank as he was told,
And never let his soup get cold.

But one day, one cold winter's day,
He threw away the spoon and screamed:

"O take the nasty soup away!
I won't have any soup to-day:

I will not, will not eat my soup!
I will not eat it, no!"

Next day! Now look, the picture shows;
How lank and lean Augustus grows!

Yet, though he feels so weak and it,
The naughty fellow cries out still

"not any soup for me, I say!
O take the nasty soup away!

I will not, will not eat my soup!
I will not eat it, no!"

The third day comes. O what a sin!
To make himself so pale and thin.

Yet, when the soup is put on the table,
He screams, as loud as he is able

"Not any soup for me, I say!
O take the nasty soup away!

I won't have any soup to-day!"

Look at him, now the fourth day's come!
He scarce outweighs a sugar-plum;

He's like a little bit of thread;
And on the fifth day, he was dead.

Humorously, yet realistically, the poem illustrates the important saying, "Seven days without the Word of God makes one weak." Not only do we become weak from denying ourselves spiritual food, but we must be aware of a time of famine, a drought of hearing God's Word. The prophet Amos paints a vivid, ominous portrait of this famine, *"'The days are coming,' declares the Sovereign Lord, 'when I will send a famine through the land—not a famine of food or a thirst for water, but a **famine of hearing the words of the Lord**'"* (Amos 8:11). Commentator J.A. Motyer stimulates our thoughts with these words:

> These things are for our learning. Have we got a Bible still in our hands? Let us prize it, read it and commit its precious truths to heart and mind. It is not an inalienable possession; it may not be ours for ever. Is the Bible still preached in our church? Let us love to hear the Word of God; let us be urgent to bring others within earshot of it. It is not our guaranteed privilege; the voice of the preacher could be silenced. The truth of God is our only fence against error. In this as in everything else the way of strength is to keep close to God and to fear much, much more the peril of falling out of His power and truth than of falling into the power and error of Satan.[13]

So, we ask ourselves: Am I training my ear to listen to the voice of Jesus in the noise of life? Am I surrendering my desires to the Lord? Am I feeding regularly on God's Word? When I hear the Word of God, am I aligning myself to do the Word of God?

TRAVEL LIGHTLY IN THE MAZE

The challenge before us is to listen with the intent to do what God says, to leave behind anything that would take the place in our hearts that only God deserves, and to continually walk in step with the Savior. As we travel the corridors of the maze and begin to apply these principles of willingness, the challenge to us is: travel lightly! To travel lightly we are to put aside anything that would weight us down and any sin that could trip us up.[14]

So faith comes from hearing,
and hearing through the word of Christ.
Romans 10:17 ESV

The maze is well traveled, and through the ages many have taken this Step of Willingness not knowing where their adventure with the Savior will lead them. Martin and Gracia Burnham are two such individuals who took the Step of Willingness and were never the same as the result.

Martin and Gracia were missionaries to the Philippines for a number of years. Martin was a pilot flying in supplies to remote areas, assisting missionary personnel in moving from place to place, and using his piloting skills any way God chose. Gracia would support him through radio navigation, home-schooling their three children, and leading Bible studies.

Their wedding anniversary was approaching, and Gracia felt it would be a good year to celebrate in a memorable way. This anniversary would prove to be more memorable than the Burnhams would bargain for. Just as Martin returned from a trip to the States, Gracia planned to whisk him away and splurge on a stay at a Filipino resort.

Their peaceful, sound sleep was rudely interrupted by boisterous yelling and loud pounding on the doors. Soon, the door to the Burnham's room burst open and members of the Abu Sayyaf terrorist group wasted no time in kidnapping the Americans. They would be held hostage along with several other individuals who were staying at the resort. The Abu Sayyaf hoped to receive money from "rich Americans" and turn the ransom into funding for their terroristic activity throughout the Philippines. As missionaries the Burnhams had little money, and the mission organization would not pay a ransom to terrorists.

In captivity for slightly over a year, the Burnhams would traipse throughout the hills, valleys, and jungles of the Philippines. Martin and Gracia lacked food, sanitary conditions, slept under the stars, and continually feared for their lives. On several occasions gun fights would ensue and rescue attempts would be made. Unfortunately, during one of these attempts Martin's life would be taken by the gunshots and Gracia would sustain a gunshot wound to the leg. However, she would be rescued and return to the States.

In only a way God could orchestrate, today Gracia travels and speaks of her ordeal and her relationship with Christ. She has ministered to thousands and even seen one of their Islamic captors came to saving faith in Jesus Christ. Martin's life and words live on. Just four short days before his kidnapping Martin shared with his home church in Kansas how he took the Step of Willingness to follow Jesus Christ. His statement revealed his heart, reflected his life, and is a tremendous call to us to take the Step of Willingness. Martin said, "I wasn't called to the Philippines. I was just called to follow Christ and that's what I'm doing."[15]

> I wasn't called to the Philippines. I was just called to follow Christ and that's what I'm doing.
> **MARTIN BURNHAM**

The Burnhams' lives are a motivation for us to have the ear of attentiveness and the heart of abandonment, which will move us to a place where our feet are aligned with the steps of God's Word. It is a place where our will is as neutral as possible so God can move it wherever He wants.

Tozer describes this as "the blessedness of nothing" and how it is the catalyst to take the Step of Willingness. "He [Abraham] had everything, *but he possessed nothing. There is the spiritual secret. There is the sweet theology of the heart which can be learned only in the school of renunciation [abandonment].*"[16] Let us take time to contemplate Tozer's prayer and help us join Abram in "the blessedness of nothing."

> Father, I want to know Thee, but my cowardly heart fears to give up its toys. I cannot part with them without inward bleeding, and I do not try to hide from Thee the terror of the parting. I come trembling, but I do come. Please root from my heart all those things which I have cherished so long and which have become a very part of my living self, so that Thou may enter and dwell there without a rival. Then shall Thou make the place of Thy feet glorious. Then shall my heart have no need of the sun to shine in it, for Thyself wilt be the light of it, and there shall be no night there. In Jesus' name. Amen.[17]

We never know where the Step of Willingness will take us in the maze of life. What we do know is that in the next chapter we will encounter an obstinate wall which will put us face-to-face with perhaps the most demanding step in the maze, the Step of Obedience.

MY VOLUNTOLD STEP

THE VOLUNTOLD STEP

➤ How does the call to follow Jesus sometimes seem like being "Voluntold?"

➤ How does Jeremiah 10:23 tie into the Step of Willingness?

LORD, I know that people's lives are not their own; it is not for them to direct their steps.

JEREMIAH 10:23

➢ Lord, this is an area I am having a hard time being **willing** in right now:

MY STEP OF WILLINGNESS

➤ The Step of Willingness Means We Have an Ear of Attention.

Listen closely, Israel, and be careful to obey...
DEUTERONOMY 6:3A (NLT)

➤ What are three practical ways you can *"pay attention in order to understand and then to put into practice"* what God's Word says?

➢ The Step of Willingness Means We Have a Heart of Abandonment.

For people everywhere report how you welcomed us and how you turned to God from idols to serve the living and true God.

1 THESSALONIANS 1:9 (NET)

An idol is anything or anybody in our life that is in the place that only Jesus deserves.

➢ We may not worship idols of stone or wood but what are two things that take the place that only Jesus deserves in your life? Be honest with yourself and the Lord!

➢ The Step of Willingness Means We Have the Feet of Alignment.

The Lord had said to Abram, "Go"

GENESIS 12:1A

The word "Go" means *"determinedly disassociating oneself."*

➢ When you are aligning yourself with God's will, what does it look like in your life to ***determinedly disassociate oneself?***

MY PERSONAL STEP OF WILLINGNESS

➢ Right now, this is where I need to take the Step of Willingness:

➢ In regard to the above, Lord I pray that: (check all that apply)

❒ You would make me willing to take the Step of Willingness.

❒ You would take my fears and anxieties as I take the Step of Willingness.

❒ You would forgive me of my pride and making my own efforts as I take the Step of Willingness.

❒ You would allow me to trust you alone in my Step of Willingness.

❒ Other:

MY PRAYER OF WILLINGNESS

➤ Reread Tozer's prayer *"The Blessedness of Possessing Nothing."*
Underline a word, phrase, or sentence that you would like to
remember from the prayer.

> Father, I want to know Thee, but my cowardly heart fears to give
> up its toys. I cannot part with them without inward bleeding, and
> I do not try to hide from Thee the terror of the parting. I come
> trembling, but I do come. Please root from my heart all those
> things which I have cherished so long and which have become
> a very part of my living self, so that Thou may enter and dwell
> there without a rival. Then shall Thou make the place of Thy feet
> glorious. Then shall my heart have no need of the sun to shine
> in it, for Thyself wilt be the light of it, and there shall be no night
> there. In Jesus' name. Amen.

➤ Write below your own *"Prayer of The Blessedness of Possessing
Nothing."* Then pray it back to the LORD.

MY SAVIOR'S STEP
OF WILLINGNESS

---

*No one takes it away from me; I give my own
life freely. I have the right to give my life,
and I have the right to take it back. This is
what my father commanded me to do.*

JOHN 10:18 (NCV)

CHAPTER 2
THE 4-LETTER WORD STEP

AN UNUSUAL WORD FOR THE MAZE

FOUR-LETTER WORDS ARE EVERY-WHERE! WE hear them at work. We see them on walls in our communities. We read them in articles. We find them floating around our schools. We note that they saturate our media. We might even discover them invading our homes. Yet, there may be more to "four-letter words" than meets the eye.

On the desk of our minds, we see the infamous book **BADEW.**[1] It is still opened to the word "Voluntold." We thumb back to the front of the book and find the definition for "four-letter words." The **BADEW** informs us they seem to fall loosely into three categories: the good, the bad, and the ugly. In the **good** sense there are a number of four-letter words that are not used in a vulgar or obscene manner. Some examples would be obey, love, or work. A quick search of the Internet reveals "good" four-letter word sites that help you find these words, e.g. unscrambling four-letter words, also four-letter words for Scrabble, and four-letter words that begin with each of the 26 letters of the alphabet. For the **bad** four-letter words, a dictionary definition will be borrowed: "The phrase **four-letter word** refers to a set of English-language words written with four letters which are considered profane, including common popular or slang terms for excretory functions, sexual activity and genitalia, terms relating to Hell or damnation when used outside of religious contexts or slurs."[2] And the **ugly** four-letter words do not necessarily fall into the good or bad categories, and can be subjective, but are not the best or most appropriate words to use in a situation. There can be varying opinions on all three categories but typically more so in this "ugly" four-letter word category.

Typically, when it comes to four-letter words the "bad" word category comes to mind. Definitely, we will hear those words or see them written when individuals are angry, frustrated, disillusioned, or even surprised or excited. However, as we make the trek across the bridge to begin the four-letter word step, we have a foreshadowing of three "good four-letter words" we want to discuss. The first one is obey. When we seek to follow Jesus and to do the Father's will we must obey. It is hard because on some level each of us finds obedience going against the grain of our nature. The second one is love. Interestingly, love is a four-letter word, and the Word of God says if we want to show Jesus we love Him, we must obey His commands.[3] The third word is work. We will recognize that it takes work on our part as Christians to demonstrate our love through obedience. Also, when we love God and obey Him, we will produce good works. These good works are not to produce salvation but are a result of our salvation. We recognize these three words are interwoven together like a carefully knitted scarf. But for this step we want to focus on an acronym for the good ole' four-letter word "obey." This Step of Obedience is not an easy one, but is a needful one as we follow Jesus throughout the maze and to His will.

I thought about my ways and turned
my steps back to Your decrees.
Psalm 119:59 (HCSB)

TAKE THE STEP OF OBEDIENCE INTO THE MAZE

So Abram went, as the Lord had told him; and Lot went with him. Abram was seventy-five years old when he set out from Harran. He took his wife Sarai, his nephew Lot, all the possessions they had accumulated and the people they had acquired in Harran, and they set out for the land of Canaan, and they arrived there.

Genesis 12:4–5

THE STEP OF OBEDIENCE MEANS WE FOLLOW GOD EVEN WHEN IT SEEMS ODD.

So Abram went, as the Lord had told him...

Genesis 12:4a

For several years, the doldrums and blahs of an Indianapolis winter or early spring would find themselves chased away by a stampeding herd of teenagers. On the chosen Saturday night, the church's youth room would rival any buzzing beehive. The streets, places of business, and church members' homes would never be the same as the storm of hormones rushed in, by, and through them. Even parents of teens would arise from their dormant winter state to voluntarily join in the mayhem.

It was a fun outreach that we called "Mission Impossible." The students would gather and be placed on a team known as "Agent Viper," "Agent Wolverine," etc. A youth volunteer or two, and myself would appear on a video requesting the team of agents to make contact with us as quickly as possible. We were hidden somewhere in the city of Indianapolis, but they needed to be very be careful of counter-enemy agents. Each Agent (a group of students) would receive clues leading them from one check point to the next to eventually locate us. Once they found us, we would let them know where our headquarters was located.

At the headquarters we would have great food, a lot of fun, and a teen-ager would share of his or her story with Jesus Christ.

This event reminds me of Abram because in the beginning the students would have no idea where they were going or where they would end up. They received a clue that led them to the next clue that led them to the next clue, and eventually the final destination. Abram's first clue was to "go." As he took this Step of Obedience, Abram received what he needed for the next step and the next step until eventually he reached his final destination, the land of Canaan.

Another parallel between Abram's travels and our youth event is this: even though the adventure was a mystery and at times the clues were hard to figure out, it was our desire for the students to figure out the clues and arrive at the final destination. If they were really stuck, we even had a hot line for the Agents to call. It usually had one of the creators of the clues at the "headquarters" to assist. We have the Word of God to read for clues and a hot line of prayer to speak with the One who wants us to find our way through the maze to the final destination. His name is Jesus Christ.

As we walk with Abram through the passageway of obedience, we gain incredible understanding from the writer of the book of Hebrews when he informs us that this obedience was odd, *"By faith Abraham, when called to go to a place he would later receive as his inheritance, **obeyed and went, even though he did not know where he was going"** (Hebrews 11:8). I can just imagine this conversation between Abram and Sarai! Abram exclaims excitedly, "Sarai, God is calling us to move and so we are going!" Lovingly, Sarai replies, "That's great honey! Where are we going?" With less enthusiasm and a sheepish look Abram states, "I don't know." Then with a shout of hope Abram says, "But God will let us know when we get there!" I can envision the same conversation with my wife not going so well, but in her defense I'm not sure if I would have the faith Abram had to jump first and ask questions later. This is why both Abram and Sarai are in the hall of faith, but as we will learn from them, there is hope for us to be men and women of faith also.

> **Lord, whatever you may ask
> of me today or in the future,
> my answer is YES!**

When we sense God leading us, we need to respond even if it seems odd, weird, or even peculiar. Because some will taunt us that this is blind and unfounded faith, it will necessitate a more careful look at the object of our faith.

Many individuals believe in belief. It is probably most obvious at sporting events. In the bottom of the ninth, fans turn their hats inside out believing this will create what is needed to make their team score enough runs to win the baseball game. The fourth quarter of the football game comes, and in spite of the freezing cold, snow, or ice, we see individuals stripping off their jackets and shirts because they believe that this semi-frozen state will give their team the needed advantage to pull out a victory. Other times the camera pans the crowd and we see signs that simply declare, "Believe." What they mean by those signs is that by believing hard enough or with enough sincerity we can make it happen. Now, I'm not saying these "superstitions" and cheering for your team are not tempting. Interestingly, when halftime comes and my favorite basketball team is not doing so well, I've found myself drifting off to the back closet. There I succumb to the tug to put on my "lucky" shirt with the school's mascot. I believe this change in wardrobe will influence the team's performance more than the coach's well-designed halftime speech or rant.

Not only do we see this at sporting events, but we also find this creeping into our walk with the LORD. We do not have a blind, subjective faith that believes in belief, but we have a rational, objective faith, which puts its confidence in Jesus Christ. These faiths are in stark contrast to each another because of the **object of the faith**. That too may seem odd.

Once again, the Indianapolis winter teaches us a lesson. It teaches us that God is a reliable and trustworthy object of our faith. The snow finally stopped. Because of Dave's caring and giving character, he found himself out in the elements clearing off family members' driveways and sidewalks with his snow blower. As snow blowers will do, Dave's jammed. As people with big hearts and a desire to get the job done tend to do, they act before they think. Dave stuck his hand in the snow blower to unjam it. The good news is that it worked. The bad news is that it worked. When the snow loosened and the snow blower resumed its blade rotation, Dave's fingers were caught in the wrong place at the wrong time.

> Obey God and leave all the consequences to Him and watch God work.
> **CHARLES STANLEY, PASTOR**

Curiosity got the best of me when I visited Dave in the ER. His hand was under a towel and I pulled it back revealing three mangled fingers. After my "examination" was complete, I asked him, "Dave, I'm your friend and you trust me, don't you?" His puzzled reply was, "Yeah." Then I proceeded to ask him, "Since you believe in me, why don't you let me perform the operation on your hand?" Suddenly, the room was filled with the awkwardness of being hugged, kissed, and doted on by that great aunt you don't remember ever meeting. Throughout this consultation, the hospital had a hand specialist waiting on duty for just such emergencies. He was a surgeon who just that day had performed a similar surgery and successfully repaired another individual's bite marks from the snow blower monster.

Dave knew me and trusted me. We were good friends and had enjoyed sharing life's experiences together, but I had (and still have) no clue about performing surgery of any kind, much less delicate hand surgery. No matter how much Dave believed in me, I was only going to make matters worse. The doctor trained and experienced in hand surgery was the one for this job. Though Dave had never met him before that day, to his credit Dave put his confidence in that surgeon. Dave lost parts of two fingers, but the surgery was a success and he returned to his lifestyle of giving. Oh, by the way, his giving no longer included using his hand to unjam snow blowers.

The point is clearly obvious and incredibly important. ***The object of our faith is critical.*** Dave could have "believed" all he wanted in me, but that would have been subjective and disastrous. He chose to believe in the hand doctor based on his objective credentials and expertise.

Likewise, Abram did not believe in any ole' god or whim or the belief to just believe; he placed his trust in the LORD God Almighty. This is why it is vital to our spiritual health to get to know God intimately and willingly through His Word, so we can take the first step toward the final destination without knowing all the "whys" and "hows." It may be odd, but all we need to know is God said go and leave. It has been said, "Faith is only as reliable and helpful as the trustworthiness of its object; and Christian faith is powerful and effective because the object of faith, Jesus Christ, is infinitely powerful and absolutely dependable. **Christian faith never fails, because the One in whom that faith is placed never fails.**"[4] This is why we must know who our God is and not rely on idols, ourselves, or anything else, just as Abram modeled for us.

THE STEP OF OBEDIENCE MEANS WE FOLLOW GOD EVEN WHEN WE ARE BAD.

> So Abram went, as the Lord had told him;
> and Lot went with him.
>
> **Genesis 12:4b**

On the surface this may seem like an unusual principle when it comes to obedience, but consider what the world's wisest man, King Solomon, pointed out for us, *"For there is not one truly righteous person on the earth who continually does good and never sins"* (Ecclesiastes 7:20 NET). In Romans 3:10–11,[5] the Apostle Paul elaborates on this concept by giving us these clear statements about our sin nature: *"As it is written: 'There is no one righteous, not even one; there is no one who understands; there is no one who seeks God.'"* We are sinners by nature and by choice. In spite of this,

God chooses to work in and through sinful humans, just like Abram, you, and me. When we gain the tiniest glimpse of His grace, it will motivate us to live from the place of victory that we have in Jesus Christ.

> So you also should consider yourselves to be dead to the power of sin and alive to God through Christ Jesus. Do not let sin control the way you live; do not give in to sinful desires. Do not let any part of your body become an instrument of evil to serve sin. Instead, give yourselves completely to God, for you were dead, but now you have new life. So use your whole body as an instrument to do what is right for the glory of God. Sin is no longer your master, for you no longer live under the requirements of the law. Instead, you live under the freedom of God's grace. (Romans 6:11–14 NLT)

The reason we want to grasp a better understanding of our sin and God's grace is because even in mid-stride of the Step of Obedience, we will stumble, and we will sin. But we do not stop, quit, or hesitate to follow Jesus as we navigate through the maze of life because the Step of Obedience does not mean "the step of perfection" but "the step of direction." Even if we take three steps forward and two steps back, the question before us is, "Are we moving toward Jesus?"

Abram sinned. At times, he was "bad" as he worked his way through the maze. At one point Abram bowed his knee to other gods, yet the true, living God called him to leave those idols behind and follow Him as we noted from Joshua 24:2–3.

> Partial obedience is really only disobedience made to look acceptable.
>
> **BILL ARNOLD**

In the difficult, narrow places in the maze, Abram's default button was set to lie. To protect himself, twice we are told Abram lied about his wife by saying she was his sister. Sarai was his half-sister, and her dad was Abram's uncle. But God viewed this as a lie. Though it might be what we call a "little white lie," God called it a "big black lie." Each of us has a default button we push or pet sin we let out of its cage when the pressures in the maze become strong. Our times of sin need to cause us to run to the Lord, experience His grace, ask for forgiveness, and take even a shaky, tiny Step of Obedience toward God.

At this moment, the walls of our maze may be closing in on us as we face the circumstances surrounding obedience. God is constantly working to make our heart of obedience purer and purer so along the path we need to experience the marvelous, matchless gift of God's forgiveness. Certainly, one of the most reassuring and powerful verses about God's incredible forgiveness is depicted for us in John's first letter. The prescription for our sin is as follows: Read 1 John 1:9 slowly and thoughtfully as many times as needed until God's forgiveness becomes a cup of refreshing cool water on a hot sultry day.

If we confess our sins, he is faithful and just to forgive us
our sins and to cleanse us from all unrighteousness.
1 John 1:9 (ESV)

There is no better "real life in the maze" example of disobedience and obedience working together to accomplish God's will and demonstrate God's forgiveness than Monessa's story.[6] Monessa and her family moved from out of state and began attending our church. Monessa's involvement in our youth group soon revealed an interesting fact about this season of her life. Monessa was pregnant. Previously, Monessa and her family had strayed from walking with the Lord, and she made a life changing decision to disobey God's will in her relationship with her boyfriend. But this was a dead-end God used in the story of Monessa and her family. She broke up with her boyfriend, the family moved, they became active in our church, and Monessa even went on the youth group's mission trip to Mexico.

The pregnancy played a significant role in turning the whole family around, and now the parents and her brother are faithfully serving the

Lord. As for Monessa, the spunky young lady that God would not give up on, is married to a loving husband, has been blessed with more children, and even enjoys being a grandmother. God did not want or cause Monessa and her family to sin, but He shined His light into the darkest corner of their maze to give them light for the next step. Today each of them is a demonstration of God's grace as they faithfully carry God's light to assist other travelers in the maze.

> Because of grace, God chose to clean up what we messed up.[7]
>
> **ANDY STANLEY, AUTHOR**

THE STEP OF OBEDIENCE MEANS WE FOLLOW GOD WHEN WE GIVE EVERYTHING.

> Abram was seventy-five years old when he set out from Harran. He took his wife Sarai, his nephew Lot, all the possessions they had accumulated and the people they had acquired in Harran, and they set out for the land of Canaan,
>
> **Genesis 12:4b–5a**

Our struggle with the 4-Letter Word Step of Obedience puts each of us at the top of a tall cliff with the hiker who got too close to the edge of the cliff and slipped off. As he began a free fall, his mind raced. It told him the drop from this height onto the jagged rocks and rough waters below would end in his demise. Across the screen of his mind flashed pictures of family, friends, good times, and regrets when suddenly he hit something. His instincts caused him to reach out, and he grabbed a hold of a branch that was sticking out of the side of the cliff. His brain quickly changed from preparing to die, to trying to live. A quick surveillance of the situation identified two troubling facts. First, hanging from that branch, he could not climb back to the top of the cliff because it was too steep. Second, hanging from that branch, he was still too high to let go without a fall taking his life. So, he did the only thing he could, he prayed, and then yelled for help.

"Help! Help! Is there anyone up there that can help me?" After a few moments of silence, a voice answered him, "This is God! I am here and I will help you!" The man now began to experience relief and renewed hope. "Lord, what do I need to do?" God replied, "Do you trust me?" "Yes, with all my heart!" blurted out the man beginning to get impatient. The Lord said to the man hanging from the branch, "Then, let go of the branch." After thinking for a few minutes about the Lord's instructions, the man yelled again, "Is anybody else up there?"

As we take the Step of Obedience and God asks us to give him everything, it feels a bit like He is asking us to "let go of the branch." Here is where we rejoin Abram in our venture. As we hang beside him on the branch, we carefully note the thread of connection between verse one and verse four. In verse one, God asks Abram to "leave" by determinately disassociating himself from his country, his people and his father's household. In verse four, we find that Abram has let go of the branch because it tells us, "So Abram left, as the LORD had told him." Abram's legacy of faith is beginning to emerge as he takes the 4-letter word step of **OBEY**. As we follow Abram in the maze, he stops, turns to look at us, and yells back "Obey," then "Come on" as he disappears behind the next wall.

Then let go of the branch!

Stepping around the corner, we find Abram is there to notify us that obey merges into another 4-letter word, **LOVE**. The apostle John, who is identified as the disciple Jesus loved,[8] is another friend we meet along the way. He personally knows of God's love and how we can love Jesus. In his gospel, John straightforwardly declares to us that when we obey Jesus we are telling Him we love Him, *"If you love me, keep my commands"* (John 14:15). In his first letter, John reiterates this when he proclaims: *"In fact, this is love for God: to keep his commands. And his commands are* *not burdensome"* (1 John 5:3). God's love language is obedience. This is how we say, "Jesus, I love you!"

The 4-letter word of obey leads to an expression of love and the 4-letter word of love guides us to another 4-letter word: WORK. Our love for the Lord will not be mere talk or pretense, but genuine love will produce authentic actions. Again, in his letter John addresses this fact, *"Dear children, let us not love with words or speech but with actions and in truth"* (1 John 3:18). Together this action of work and love will be evident by what we do.

So intertwined are obedience and faith that you cannot have one without the other. Dietrich Bonhoeffer, a German Pastor and theologian,[9] expressed this beautifully when he stated, "Only he who he who believes is obedient; only he who is obedient believes."[10] This correlation between giving everything and obedient faith is clear, and James cites Abram as a vivid example.

> Was not our father Abraham considered righteous for what he did when he offered his son Isaac on the altar? You see that his faith and his actions were working together, and his faith was made complete by what he did. And the scripture was fulfilled that says, "Abraham believed God, and it was credited to him as righteousness," and he was called God's friend. You see that a person is considered righteous by what they do and not by faith alone. (James 2:21–24)

THE STEP OF OBEDIENCE MEANS WE FOLLOW GOD WHEN WE ARE YIELDED.

and they arrived there

Genesis 12:5b

Whew! We all know what it is like to finish a looooong trip. Certainly, Abram and Sarai were overjoyed to finally be at their new home. It was a journey that started as a mystery trip, included a layover in a place called Haran, and finally after many frequent-walker-miles they came into their new land. The narrator of Abram's account, Moses, flatly states: "they arrived there." At least it seems to us like a band, balloons, celebratory streamers, and a throng of people should welcome our heroes to their final destination. But there was none of that because Abram was yielded to an obedient journey in the maze that is a *"walk of faith and not sight."*[11] In many ways this step of yielded obedience and faith was just the first of many tricky and dangerous turns in his life's maze because, *"Abram was looking forward to the city with foundations, whose architect and builder is God."* (Hebrews 11:10).

Hebrews 11, also known as the "Hall of Faith," tells us about the faith of Abram, Sarai, and their immediate descendants: Isaac, Jacob, and Joseph. Many other men and women are cited for their yielded obedience throughout the chapter, but the writer concludes the chapter with one of the most astonishing statements in all the Scriptures: *"These were all commended for their faith, **yet none of them received what had been promised**, since God had planned something better for us so that only together with us would they be made perfect"* (Hebrews 11:39–40). They walked by faith all their lives, but it was only in heaven and with us that the promise is completely fulfilled and realized. We may never fully realize the implications of this outside of heaven, but what we know is that the light of Abram's life gives us much needed guidance for the next step in our daily maze.

A story of incredible yielded obedience is told of Alexander the Great who at the time was conquering the then-known world. He approached a city fortified by great stone walls and mighty fighting men. He marched right up to the gate, demanded to see the king, and requested that they surrender to him and his army immediately. The king laughed at Alexander the Great and the small army that was accompanying him. "We shall never surrender to you!" shouted the King. Upon hearing that declaration of defiance, Alexander the Great barked orders to his troops. His men formed a single file line and began to march. Staying in cadence the little band of soldiers made their way towards a cliff which had a sharp drop of hundreds of feet. As the men advanced toward the cliff, the King thought surely Alexander the Great will order his men to stop because the fall from the cliff would mean certain death. But he did no such thing. Instead, one-by-one the men marched right off the edge of the cliff to their death. About half a dozen men marched to their death as they yielded their lives to obey Alexander's orders; then he gave the order to halt. Alexander the Great came back to the King and requested again that the village surrender to him. This time the king and the whole town yielded to Alexander the Great and his army because they knew with this kind of awesome obedience there was nothing these men would not do for Alexander the Great. We want to have this same kind of yielded obedience with our Lord.

LOVE DEEPLY IN THE MAZE

"The 4-Letter Word Step" has produced for us four mini steps that further flesh out what it means to obey. Let's review them: Odd, Bad, Everything, and Yield. These might seem a bit forced but that is intentional because as they come together they form the acronym **O.B.E.Y.** Remember to obey leads us to another 4-letter word, love. To demonstrate a deep love for Jesus Christ is the intent of the Step of Obedience. The purer our motives are to obey Jesus, the louder our lives will say, "Jesus, I love You."

> If you love me, you will obey what I command.[12]
> *JESUS*

Many times, we wish God would give us a call, send us a letter, shoot us a text, or an email to say: "This is my will for you now. This is where I want you to be in five years, and this is what I want you doing in ten years." Rarely does God do this because we would struggle with believing Him or we might back out if we knew where God was taking us. God says, "Take the next Step of Obedience and then I will know your love for me right where you are in the maze."

Several years ago, I had what I would consider a "letter in the mail from God" experience. Though I have always wanted God to send me His will in a letter, I did not handle this particular instance well, but it serves to help illustrate each letter in O.B.E.Y.

My wife and I were having serious questions and difficult decisions to make about the ministry in which we were then serving. There were several concerns about the church's leadership and direction of the church, but we sensed that we were on the verge of God doing something great in the youth ministry. As we prayed and talked about it, we decided that God wanted us to be willing to continue to minister to the youth in that location with His sustaining perseverance and by His grace.

> Only he who believes is obedient;
> only he who is obedient believes.
> **DIETRICH BONHOEFFER, PASTOR**

Shortly thereafter, and completely from left field or in this case North Dakota, I received an envelope in the mail. It was from another church that wanted to know if I would be interested in serving in their congregation. I was dumbfounded, flabbergasted, and all those other funny expressions of disbelief! We had just told God that we were willing to stay and continue to minister in a difficult situation, and now God sends His "letter from heaven."

The Step of Obedience was playing out right before our eyes. This Step of Obedience was **odd**. The timing was odd. The location was odd. My wife and I had just wrestled and settled in our minds what we thought God wanted. We had placed our confidence in Him as the object of our faith. But in this Step of Obedience, I was **bad**. Much to my chagrin, I did not fill out the questionnaire and did not do much by way of inquiry into that ministry. God put this opportunity in my lap, and I did very little to respond by taking the Step of Obedience. In spite of my lack of action, God has since taught me to examine closely the opportunities He brings my way, for they are a significant part in my Christlike development. To take this Step of Obedience, we would have had to give up **everything** much like Abram did. We would have moved to a new location, moving from one cold environment to an even colder one. We would have had to give up good friends, an established ministry, and live further from parents. We felt we had just **yielded** ourselves to God to obey by staying and facing a difficult situation, but God was more interested in our having ongoing yielded wills.

All four of the mini steps of obedience played a part in God's outworking of His will. It wasn't as clear as I'd like for it to have been. From my perspective, it seemed messy. I didn't do everything correctly, and I felt that once I yielded to the Lord, He turned around and asked me to yield again. God continually puts us in positions to see if we will obey what we know to do and will we give everything to Him. I learned a valuable lesson in following the Savior in the sticky situations of the maze. In the end, my wife and I made headway in our maze of life and God used the outcome in a lot of individual's lives. Life may not seem like it dots all the "*I*s" and crosses all the "*T*s," but we can find comfort in the fact that God will not rest until His work is completed. *"And I am certain that God, who began the good work within you, will continue his work until it is finally finished on the day when Christ Jesus returns"* (Philippians 1:6 NLT).

> The greatest test of life
> is obedience to God.
>
> **EZRA TAFT BENSON**

We will not know what the future holds and we will probably not get a phone call or a letter from God by way of North Dakota. If we want to be where God wants us to be in five years and doing what God wants us to be doing in ten years, then we need to do today what we know He wants us to do. This moment in time is all we have. If God gives you tomorrow, do what he wants tomorrow and the next day and the next. If we do each day what God wants us to do, then in five years we will be where God wants us, doing the thing God wants us to do.

One of the four elements of obedience is a foundational stone for each of the steps we will take with Abram along the way, but perhaps it is no bigger than at the base of our next step, *The Martyr's Step*. As we take the Step of Obedience and demonstrate our love for the Lord, God will ask for us to die to self in every area of our lives. God is actively at work to not only have us die to ourselves but also to live for Jesus Christ, which is the next step; the Step of Wholeheartedness.

MY 4-LETTER WORD STEP

THE 4-LETTER WORD STEP

➢ How does the instruction to obey Jesus sometimes seem like a "4-Letter Word?"

➢ What does Psalm 119:59 teach you about the Step of Obedience?

*I thought about my ways and turned
my steps back to Your decrees.*

PSALM 119:59 (HCSB)

➢ This is an area I am having a hard time being **obedient** in
right now:

THE STEP OF OBEDIENCE — O.B.E.Y.

➢ This seems **Odd** to me about God's will for me right now:

➢ The Word of God tells me I'm **Bad**, that I am a sinner.

Psalm 103:8–12 tells us about God's incredible forgiveness. Read the verses below, then

1) underline two statements about God's forgiveness that stand out to you;

2) spend a couple of minutes thanking God for His forgiveness to you personally;

3) share what you learned about God's forgiveness with a family member or friend.

The Lord is compassionate and gracious,
slow to anger, abounding in love.
He will not always accuse,
nor will he harbor his anger forever;
he does not treat us as our sins deserve
or repay us according to our iniquities.
For as high as the heavens are above the earth,
so great is his love for those who fear him;
as far as the east is from the west,
so far has he removed our transgressions from us.

PSALM 103:8–12

➢ For Abram to give **Everything** to the Lord, his faith and obedience were intertwined.

Read James 2:21–24 to review how Abram's faith and obedience were connected.

Was not our father Abraham considered righteous for what he did when he offered his son Isaac on the altar? You see that his faith and his actions were working together, and his faith was made complete by what he did. And the scripture was fulfilled that says, "Abraham believed God, and it was credited to him as righteousness," and he was called God's friend. You see that a person is considered righteous by what they do and not by faith alone.

JAMES 2:21–24

What does this connection of faith and obedience mean for your life right now?

➤ Obedience demands us to be **Yielded** regardless of the outcome.

---

*These were all commended for their faith, **yet none
of them received what had been promised**, since
God had planned something better for us so that
only together with us would they be made perfect.*
HEBREWS 11:39–40

**Though these verses could seem to be discouraging,
how are they intended to encourage you to yield to
the Lord in life's maze?**

MY PERSONAL STEP OF OBEDIENCE

➢ From what you noted already, what is an area that I need to step out in faith and obedience?

➢ If I am honest about this area, I am trusting in my:

- ❐ Self
- ❐ Friends/family
- ❐ Financial security
- ❐ Position
- ❐ Possessions
- ❐ Lord Jesus Christ
- ❐ Other:

➢ What did the story of Dave and the snow blower teach you about the **object of your faith** and its importance?

MY PRAYER OF OBEDIENCE

➢ In order to take the **Step of Obedience**, right now God wants me to do this:

➢ Write a prayer below that expresses your desire to obey the LORD or your struggle to obey Him. Be honest with the LORD; He already knows your thoughts. Then pray it back to the LORD.

MY SAVIOR'S STEP OF OBEDIENCE

And when he (Jesus) was living as a man, he humbled himself and was fully obedient to God, even when that caused his death—death on a cross.

PHILIPPIANS 2:8 (NCV)

CHAPTER 3

THE MARTYR'S STEP

AN UNCOMFORTABLE WORD FOR THE MAZE

THE YEARS WERE 1899 THROUGH 1901. The place was China. The movement was a Chinese uprising that terrorized imperialists, foreigners, and Christians. And the event was known as the Boxer Rebellion. These extreme Chinese nationalists were known as Boxers because they practiced a form of Chinese martial arts that incorporated boxing skills. Though officially denounced by the Chinese government, the Boxers were secretly supported by many of the royal court. We are informed that, "In the two years that the Boxers rampaged, they killed approximately 250 missionaries and nearly 30,000 Christian Chinese."[1] The story that emerges from this time of great horror is a remarkable account of wholeheartedness.

As the Boxers surrounded a mission station with one exception, they sealed off the exits. At that particular exit was an open gate where a cross was placed in the dirt. One would not be able to make his way out without stepping on or around the cross. The missionaries and students were informed that anyone who walked out of the mission station and trampled the cross would have his or her life spared. If they would not renounce their faith by stepping on the cross, they would be killed instantly.

The account describes the first seven students whose lives were saved because as they exited the compound they chose to step on the cross, thus proclaiming they were disavowing their faith in Jesus Christ. The scene radically changed when the eighth student approached the cross. It was a young girl. She stopped, knelt to pray for strength, and then carefully walked around the cross. Immediately, her life was taken, as she was shot to death. Realizing the genuine life and death consequences, the remaining students each were faced with a critical decision. Would they die to their faith and live, or would they live for their faith and die? Motivated by the courage of this young girl, the remaining 92 students also walked around the cross and to their deaths.[2] The Boxer Rebellion and these young students' courageous actions teach us an extraordinary lesson in living and dying for Jesus Christ.

The dictionary defines a martyr as "a person who is put to death or endures great suffering on behalf of any belief, principle, or cause."[3] As we open the **BADEW**,[4] we notice a dog-eared page. This well-worn page reveals the word "martyr" highlighted, being marked for emphasis, and showing signs of repeated use. **BADEW** defines a martyr as someone who gives their life for a cause. Coming from the Greek word for witness (*marturia*), we denote that a martyr is also a witness to someone or something. That individual's life and death speak as a significant testimony for what he or she believes, and as we shall see, Abram's life will speak loud and clear in the maze.

Though Abram did not die a martyr's death, he did live a martyr's life. We have noted that Abram sinned and made mistakes, yet he still gave himself wholeheartedly to God's call on his life. He was a living martyr. Abram lived his life for the cause of the Lord, and his life was a witness to that fact. Abram was willing to leave all, his faith was credited to him as righteousness, and we discover Abram gave himself completely to God's will for his life. As Abram took each of these steps, his resolve to die to himself and live for God's purpose became stronger and stronger. As we take these steps with Abram, our resolve to live for God's purpose will become stronger and stronger also.

I am reminded of a song my friend Gene Helsel wrote. It is a tremendous song that expresses what it means to follow God wholeheartedly. It speaks of our need to live near the cross, and how difficult it is to live as a martyr for Jesus by dying to ourselves. Read the lyrics of Gene's song "I Will Live":[5]

> And I want to follow Jesus
> But I know that this is what He said:
> That I must live in the shadow of the Cross
> That I must count all earthly gain but loss
> Deny myself, and embrace the pain He has for me
> And learn to live the agony of dying to myself

Let us keep these powerful lyrics in mind as Abram guides us to take the Step of Wholeheartedness in our maze.

"The Martyr's Step" is located in an out-of-the-way, unpopular path in the maze of life. Jesus speaks of this road and makes crystal clear what it means to follow Him when He states, *"If anyone wants to become my follower, he must deny himself, take up his cross daily, and follow me"* (Luke 9:23b NET). We must learn to navigate this critical step of dying to ourselves and living to Jesus with all that we have. We may not be asked to die for our Lord physically, but we are asked to live for Him daily, by learning to live the agony of dying to ourselves. In doing so, our life is a witness to the Savior both in life and in death.

My feet have closely followed his steps; I have kept to his way without turning aside.
Job 23:11

TAKE THE STEP OF WHOLEHEARTEDNESS IN THE MAZE

> He took his wife Sarai, his nephew Lot, all the possessions they had accumulated and the people they had acquired in Harran, and they set out for the land of Canaan, and they arrived there.
>
> **Genesis 12:5**

THE STEP OF WHOLEHEARTEDNESS MEANS WE BURN THE BRIDGE OF RETURN.

> He took his wife Sarai, his nephew Lot, all the possessions they had accumulated and the people they had acquired in Harran, and they set out for the land of Canaan.
>
> **Genesis 12:5a**

Abram's story gives us light to see down the next passageway, and it gives us an invaluable example for this Step of Wholeheartedness. Together with Abram, we come to a third significant intersection in the maze of life. As with each of the turns in the maze, we cannot merely be bystanders. A decision must be made, and action is required. Each of our first three steps is encapsulated by three action verbs recorded for us in verses one, three, and five. At the first intersection, Abram is instructed by God to **leave** (vs.1) or willingly disassociate himself from anything that would stand in the place that only God deserves. It is the Step of Willingness. At the next turn, we watch as Abram **left** (vs.3) in obedience to God's instructions to go to a new place. It is the Step of Obedience. Now we stand at this crossroad and observe that Abram **took** (vs.5) his family, possessions, and people, which indicates he took responsibility for himself and his group.[6] This is the Step of Wholeheartedness. Before us is the challenge to join Abram in his pursuit of God, to do so with all we have, and to do so with such a commitment that we will never be the same.

Verse five informs us that Abram took his family, all the belongings he had accrued, and all the servants he had amassed in Haran. Abram left nothing behind; therefore, there was no reason for him to go back to Haran. He responded to God's call on his life with everything he had and with everything in his being. Abram's heart was now in Canaan; right where God wanted it. Walking with Abram will cause us to ask ourselves, "Where is our heart?" We must pause to reflect on what we value in our innermost thoughts, possessions, and relationships because Jesus tells us that where our treasures are, that is where our heart is also.[7] Abram was wholeheartedly devoted to the Lord, because he had given the Lord all of his treasures, which was a reflection of his heart.

At this crossroad of "Wholehearted Parkway" and "Half-hearted Boulevard," we will encounter many who are half-hearted followers of Jesus. Many who are afraid of the obstacles, the unknown, the strength of the enemy, or are battle-worn. At times, this can be a description of us as we are called by God to intentionally pursue Him with all we have. Abram did. Others have. And so can we!

The Parkway of Wholeheartedness beckons us to be sold out for Jesus, to be "all-in," not to hold anything back, and to do it now. But as we peer down the Boulevard of Half-heartedness, a desire to keep our options open raises up and shouts to us: "Something better might come along." "You might change your mind." "You can always make a commitment tomorrow." We stand at an impasse in our maze, not making a decision, and yet we have made a decision. Without a conscious decision to follow Jesus wholeheartedly into the depths of the maze, we have chosen to live a non-committed, half-hearted life on the path of Self Street. This Step of Wholeheartedness must be *intentional* and *continual*, not left to chance or inattention.

Abram "burned his bridge." He took everything he had from Haran and set out for Canaan. Abram did not leave anything behind as a temptation to go back. The concept of burning one's bridge is to eliminate the possibility of one's return to where they once were. Whatever is beneath the bridge, a deep ravine, a roaring river, a swampy marsh, it cannot be crossed without the bridge. That is why "burning one's bridge" means that we cannot or will not go back to where we were before the burning of the bridge. Sure, we could build the bridge again, but by "burning the bridge" we are saying we will not, and we will make it hard, if not impossible, for us to go back. Wholeheartedness forever changes us. We will now traverse in this new territory come what may. This is the agony of the choice to die to ourselves. Throughout our time in the maze, we need to have many of these "bridge burning moments" in order to continually live in the shadow of the cross.

> If you are Christians, be consistent.
> Be Christians out and out;
> Christians every hour, in every part.
> Be aware of half-hearted discipleship,
> of compromise with evil,
> of conformity to the world,
> of trying to serve two masters....
> **HORATIUS BONAR, COMMENTATOR**

To further motivate us to make a wholehearted decision to follow Jesus and burn the bridge of return, let us ponder the insights of the great "theologian" Theodore Geisel, better known to most by his pen name: Dr. Seuss. From his poem *The Zode*,[8] we learn the importance of making wholehearted decisions.

> Did I ever tell you about the young Zode,
>
> Who came to two signs at the fork in the road?
>
> One said to Place One, and the other, Place Two.
>
> So the Zode had to make up his mind what to do.
>
> Well...the Zode scratched his head, and his chin and his pants
>
> And he said to himself, "I'll be taking a chance
>
> If I go to Place One. Now, that place may be hot!

And so, how do I know if I'll like it or not?

On the other hand though, I'll be sort of a fool

If I go to Place Two and find it too cool.

In that case I may catch a chill and turn blue!

So, maybe Place One is the best, not Place Two,

But then again, what if Place One is too high?

I may catch a terrible earache and die!

So place Two may be best! On the other hand though...

What might happen to me if Place Two is too low?

I might get some very strange pain in my toe!

So Place One may be best," and he started to go.

Then he stopped, and he said, "On the other hand though...

On the other hand...other hand...other hand though..."

And for 36 hours and a half that poor Zode

Made starts and made stops at the fork in the road.

Saying, "Don't take a chance. No! You may not be right."

Then he got an idea that was wonderfully bright!

"Play safe!" cried the Zode. "I'll play safe. I'm no dunce!

I'll simply start out for both places at once!"

And that's how the Zode who would not take a chance

Got no place at all with a split in his pants.

This concept of burning our bridges and making wholehearted decisions to follow the LORD is nicely summarized by Russell Bertand's statement, "Nothing is so exhausting as indecision, and nothing so futile."

THE STEP OF WHOLEHEARTEDNESS MEANS WE BUILD THE BRIDGE OF RESOLVE.

and they arrived there.

Genesis 12:5b

Again, we draw attention to the small, but important and insightful phrase, *"and they arrived there."* Abram had burned his bridge behind him by taking all his belongings and people, and now they had arrived in Canaan. This Promised Land is where he will focus all of his attention and begin to build the bridge of resolve. This bridge is built with courage, decision, and determination. As we take a telescope and look down the corridor of Abram's life, six principles emerge to help us be wholeheartedly resolved to doing God's will in an ungodly culture.

> To just read the Bible, attend church, and avoid "big" sins-is this passionate, wholehearted love for God?
>
> *FRANCOIS FENELON*

First, we are determined to pursue the true God, not the gods of this culture, Genesis 12:7–8. Though Abram had worshiped other gods, that was a thing of the past for him. Now he was committed to the one, true, living God. One of the first things he did upon entering the land of Canaan was to build an altar to call on the name of the LORD, and he continued to commune with his God in the midst of a culture that followed after other gods. Our culture offers the altars of pleasure, possession, popularity, and position. Many bow to and worship those gods, but we resolve to bow only to the Lord Jesus Christ.

Second, we are determined to hold to godly convictions, not compromise for personal profit, Genesis 14:18–24. Abram went to battle in order to rescue his nephew Lot. Upon winning the war, he received the spoils of victory. Then Abram worshiped God by giving a tenth of the booty to God's Priest Melchizedek. The King of Sodom, who also benefited from Abram's victory, tried to persuade Abram to keep the spoils for himself. But by doing so, Abram would be indebted to the wicked King for his graciousness and advice. Even though keeping the spoils would have benefited Abram personally, he chose to honor the LORD with the treasures. Each of us must develop and hold to convictions from God and His Word, then resist the temptation to give in even if we feel pressure or would benefit personally.

Third, we are determined to have confidence in our God, not in our own works, Genesis 15:6. One of the greatest statements about Abram is that he believed God and it was credited to him as righteousness. This description of Abram is so important for us that God made note of it throughout the Scriptures (see Gen.15:6; Romans 4:3, 20–24; Gal. 3:6; James 2:23). Abram's trust was in what God would do and not what his works could accomplish. Spiritually speaking Abram's works and our works can achieve nothing. This emphasis is for us also so that we will build a bridge of confidence in the all-sufficient work of Jesus Christ and not on anything we can do to produce status or favor with God.

Fourth, we are determined to obey God's instructions, not follow our own understanding, Genesis 17:9–14. Abram was 99 when God instituted the covenant of circumcision for Abram and his descendants. This was God's promise to His people and instruction for them to follow. As a wholehearted follower of God, He may give us instructions that seem different or difficult but will build a bridge of courage to do His will and not follow our own thoughts.

Fifth, we are determined to hold onto God's promises, not focus on our timing, Genesis 21:1–5. Abram was 100 years old when Isaac was born. It was 25 years after the LORD first promised Abram he would have a son. During those years in the waiting room, Abram and Sarai decided to try to take God's timing into their own hands and help God fulfill His promise to them. This is where the idea of an heir through Hagar began to make more and more sense until they put that idea into action. We build a bridge to God's promises when we are firmly resolved to wait for His timing alone.

Sixth, we are determined to sacrifice our treasures, not hold back anything, Genesis 22:1–18. Isaac was a treasure to Abram, but God asked him to give Isaac up. As Ray Stedman, a pastor and author, discusses the gift of Isaac, he gives us this insight:

> But God's gifts are of no value until we are willing, if necessary, to let go of them so that God might reign in our lives without a rival. When we come to a place where we are willing to obey Him without question, when his will for our lives means more than anything, when we love Him with all our strength, then God will resurrect that gift within us. Through our yieldedness, He will make that gift a blessing to everyone it touches.[9]

We cannot fully build the bridge of resolve until we release to God everything in order to take the Step of Wholeheartedness.

We meet all kinds of people in life's maze, and many of them are tremendous examples for us to be committed to the Step of Wholeheartedness. One such individual is Jonathan Edwards. Jonathan Edwards (October 5, 1703–March 22, 1758) was an American revivalist, preacher, and theologian. He was instrumental in the First Great Awakening, and some of the first revivals in 1733–1735 were at his church in Northampton, Massachusetts. He drafted a document he called "Resolutions." The purpose of these 70 "Resolutions" sums up nicely our thoughts on building a bridge to wholeheartedness:

> Being sensible that I am unable to do anything without God's help, I do humbly entreat him by his grace to enable me to keep these Resolutions, so far as they are agreeable to his will, for Christ's sake. Remember to read over these Resolutions once a week.[10]

Continue to focus on the fact that for us to be resolved to follow Jesus, we need to make courageous, decisive, wholehearted decisions to live in the shadow of the cross.

PROCLAIM CONSISTENTLY IN THE MAZE

Abram's life in the maze consistently proclaims to us to take the Step of Wholeheartedness with God. His life continually proclaims to us to discover and leave behind areas of half-heartedness. Because Abram's walk in the maze is not perfect and he struggled with half-heartedness, our lives intertwine with his. This gives us hope that we too can be men and women of faith by taking this important Step of Wholeheartedness.

As followers of Jesus Christ, each of us is called to be wholehearted, whether it be in life or death. This goes beyond the willingness to burn the bridge back to our old way of thinking and doing. It is a deliberate resolution of our minds that moves with conviction into our hearts and then out into our hands and feet. We take action to build a resolve to live for Christ in life or death. We wholeheartedly pack up our belongings, leave behind those who hinder us from following Jesus, and look for a city whose architect and builder is God.

Often we see statements like: "Basketball is life. The rest is just details," which communicates that basketball is what life is all about and everything else is just to get us to our life's priority, basketball. Based on Colossians 3:1–4, the Apostle Paul's description of who we are in Christ would change the statement to: "Christ is life. The rest is just details."

> Since, then, you have been raised with Christ, set your hearts on things above, where Christ is, seated at the right hand of God. Set your minds on things above, not on earthly things. **For you died, and your life is now hidden with Christ in God.** When Christ, who is your life, appears, then you also will appear with him in glory. (Colossians 3:1–4)

We seek to live our day to day lives by the reality that our life is in Christ. *"I have been crucified with Christ. It is no longer I who live, but Christ who lives in me. And the life I now live in the flesh I live by faith in the*

Son of God, who loved me and gave himself for me" (Galatians 2:20 ESV). When we let this glorious reality of Christ in us saturate the fabric of our being, then living wholeheartedly to Christ and dying to ourselves become a natural by-product.

We may not want to give our hearts wholly to the LORD because we are afraid He will ask or make us do something we don't want to do. We may not say it this way, but our thoughts might be something like: "I don't want to give myself wholeheartedly to the LORD, because He will make me become a missionary in Africa. I don't want to be a missionary, live in Africa, or go that far from family." King David, who had his own successes and failures in the maze, gave us these words to mull over, *"Take delight in the Lord, and he will give you the desires of your heart"* (Psalm 37:4). David is not saying that God will just give us whatever our heart wants. What he is saying is that when the LORD has our heart, God will turn around and give us the desires of our heart. It is because these heart desires are now coming from the LORD.

But because my servant Caleb has a different spirit and follows me wholeheartedly, I will bring him into the land he went to, and his descendants will inherit it.
Numbers 14:24

When I was a Youth Pastor, individuals would say to me, "I could never work with teenagers." My response was "I can't think of doing anything else, and I can't believe they pay me to work with teens." The difference was that God had placed that desire in my heart and then He gave it to me. When we give our heart wholeheartedly to God, He places the desires in our heart, and then the LORD turns around and gives us the desires of our heart. Even if that means becoming a missionary to Africa. What an awesome God we have!

The following is a creed which deeply and profoundly expresses what it means to be a wholehearted follower of Jesus Christ in the maze of life. It has been reported that this writing was found in the room of a young African who had been martyred for his faith in Jesus Christ!

The Creed of a Bold Jesus Follower[11]

I am part of the fellowship of the unashamed, the die has been cast, I have stepped over the line, the decision has been made—I'm a disciple of Christ!

I won't look back, let up, slow down, back away or be still.

My past is redeemed, my present makes sense, my future is secure!

I'm finished and done with low living, sight walking, smooth knees, colorless dreams, tamed visions, worldly talk, cheap giving and dwarfed goals.

My face is set, my course is fast, my goal is heaven, my road is narrow, my way is rough, my companions are few, my guide is reliable, my mission is clear.

I won't give up, shut up, let up until I have stayed up, stored up, prayed up, for the cause of Jesus Christ.

I must go till He comes, give till I drop, preach till everyone knows, work till He stops me and when He comes for His own, He will have no trouble recognizing me because my banner will have been clear.

With this kind of resolve we will, with God's help, have the strength to survive against our cultural stream, or perhaps even reverse it. Of course, we are a minority, but armed with the promises of God we can have a spiritual impact that is greater than our numbers might suggest.

It may come down to a simple question:

"Are we willing to pay the Price?"

In the journey through the maze, we have met a number of individuals who have given their hearts completely to God; however, these individuals are just like you and me, with fears, struggles, and times of half-heartedness. We find this is true of our guide Abram and yet he is marked as a man of obedience, a paragon of faith, a friend of God, and a blessing to the nations. Abram gives more and more of himself to God by being alert to the heart and thoughts of His God known as El Shaddai, the Powerful One. In our next chapter, we will want to stay in step with Abram because he demonstrates for us how to walk closely and give careful attention to our worship and relationship with the Maker of the heavens and the earth.

MY MARTYR'S STEP

THE MARTYR'S STEP

➢ Apart from Jesus, what martyr are you familiar with? What is his/her story?

➢ How is the call to follow Jesus like being a "Martyr?"

➢ How does Job 23:11 tie into the Step of Wholeheartedness?

My feet have closely followed his [the LORD's] steps;
I have kept to his way without turning aside.

JOB 23:11

THE STEP OF WHOLEHEARTEDNESS

**The Step of Wholeheartedness
means we burn bridges of return.**

➢ What does it mean to "burn bridges" in our walk in the maze
with Jesus?

**Read the following verses. From these words of Jesus,
put in your own words what is He telling you about
burning your bridges.**

- Matthew 6:21

- Matthew 6:24

- Matthew 16:24–27

➢ In your walk with Jesus, what bridge do you need to burn
right now?

The Step of Wholeheartedness
means we build bridges of resolve.

➢ From the chapter, what was helpful to you in understanding the concept of "taking the Step of Wholeheartedness" in the maze of life?

➢ From each passage below, make an observation about what God is saying regarding following Him wholeheartedly. How would you finish the sentence?

• Galatians 2:20; Following God wholeheartedly means

• Colossians 3:1–3; Following God wholeheartedly means

• Psalm 37:4; Following God wholeheartedly means

MY PERSONAL STEP OF WHOLEHEARTEDNESS

➢ When it comes to taking the Step of Wholeheartedness, one area in my life that God wants me to deal with is:

➢ In regard to the above answer, one Step of Wholeheartedness God wants me to take is:

MY PRAYER
OF WHOLEHEARTEDNESS

➢ Read the lyrics to Gene Helsel's song "I Will Live." Circle the phrase that jumps out at you in regard to the Step of Wholeheartedness.

> And I want to follow Jesus
> But I know that this is what He said:
> That I must live in the shadow of the Cross
> That I must count all earthly gain but loss
> Deny myself, and embrace the pain He has for me
> And learn to live the agony of dying to myself

➢ Take the song, "I Will Live" and use it as a guide to write a prayer to the Lord below. Then pray it back to the LORD.

MY SAVIOR'S STEP
OF WHOLEHEARTEDNESS

Father, if you are willing, take this cup from me; yet not my will, but yours be done.

LUKE 22:42

CHAPTER 4
THE VIGILANT STEP

A UNIQUE WORD FOR THE MAZE

THE MAN ENTERING THE ROOM sported a Mohawk, a beard which was grown longer at the chin, and a shirt that was two sizes too small and could not contain the bulging muscles in his biceps and chest. One arm had a sleeve tattoo, and his gravelly, raspy voice demanded our attention as he spoke loudly and confidently. He seemed out of place for a training session on dealing with individuals struggling with mental health issues, but

he was our next speaker. However, his session seemed to last only a few minutes because of his interesting delivery, charismatic personality, and practical suggestions. Come to think of it, he was perfect for the Crisis Intervention Team training conducted at the Police Training Facility.

Mike was a well-seasoned Police officer who married a Police officer. He was completely consumed by law enforcement even though an injury had caused him to cease from active duty in the field. Because of his love for police work, Mike shared with us that in his mind he would play out scenarios of an active shooter invading whatever room or building he found himself in. He was continually alert to potential danger when he was at a restaurant, a store, a park, even while we were at the Police Training Facility.

Mike spoke from experience as he taught us to be vigilant or alert to our surroundings, but at the same time he warned us against becoming hypervigilant, which is to see a "bad guy" around every corner and behind every bush. Mike admitted that at times he went from one side to the other on the line between vigilance and hypervigilance. Overall, his training was the best of the day. It equipped me to be a better security dispatcher and instilled me with a new-found sense of vigilance or alertness.

The dictionary definition of vigilant is: 1) keenly watchful to detect danger; wary; 2) ever awake and alert; sleeplessly watchful.[1] Upon opening the **BADEW**[2] to vigilant we are met with a corny joke that draws our attention to the main focus of vigilance, *"Be alert, the world needs more lerts!"* The chief idea of vigilant is "alertness," and in the spiritual world it is "to be alert to what God is doing in and around me in my life's maze and to be sensitive to my relationship with Him." The Word of God tells us the reason, *"**Stay alert!** Watch out for your great enemy, the devil. He prowls around like a roaring lion, looking for someone to devour"* (1 Peter 5:8 NLT).

We also find a special note for hyperspiritual where **BADEW** defines it as, "Individuals who try to read into every situation and circumstance God's will." At first glance this seems like a good statement, but upon reflection it is much the same as what Mike was saying about being hypervigilant. We need to be alert to the potential dangers surrounding us, just like we want to be alert to what God is doing in our lives and our relationship with Him. However, we must not look for danger where it is not, just as we must not force Jesus into saying or doing something He is not.

A couple of examples of hyperalertness might serve us well.[3] A man was driving in Washington D.C., when his car stalled in front of the Philippine Embassy. He took that to mean that he should be a missionary to the Philippines. Or, the woman who was not sure if she should go on a trip to Israel, but one night while reading through the travel brochures and tour information, she noticed that the flight was to be on a 747. The next morning she woke up and on her digital clock the time was 747. She took that as a sign she should go on the trip to Israel. This is why it is so important to stay in step with our Lord, not running ahead of Him nor lagging behind Him.

So what does it mean to be vigilant but not hypervigilant in life's maze? We observe Abram building many altars of worship to the Lord and at times circling back around to the altars he made so he could meet and stay in step with the Lord. We glean from Abram's life that it is needful for us to have a continual heart and mind that is alert and sensitive to what God is doing in our part of the maze. This comes through regular time with Him. With this alertness to the Lord comes discernment when God is in something and when He is not. The Step of Alertness means we find our confidence in the Lord, we look for the confirmation of the Lord, and we walk in communion with the Lord.

The LORD guides our steps,
and we never know where he will lead us.
Proverbs 20:24 (ERV)

TAKE THE STEP OF ALERTNESS IN THE MAZE

Abram traveled through the land as far as the site of the great tree of Moreh at Shechem. At that time the Canaanites were in the land. The LORD appeared to Abram and said, "To your offspring I will give this land." So he built an altar there to the LORD, who had appeared to him. From there he went on toward the hills east of Bethel and pitched his tent, with Bethel on the west and Ai on the east. There he built an altar to the LORD and called on the name of the LORD.

Genesis 12:6–8

THE STEP OF ALERTNESS MEANS WE GO IN THE CONFIDENCE OF THE LORD.

> Abram traveled through the land as far as the site of the great tree of Moreh at Shechem. At that time the Canaanites were in the land.
>
> **Genesis 12:6**

Remember, at the outset, our hero Abram and his band of sojourners did not know where they were going. *"By faith Abraham, when called to go to a place he would later receive as his inheritance, obeyed and went, even though he did not know where he was going"* (Hebrews 11:8). This introduces us to the step of spiritual vigilance or "alertness" to the LORD.

At some point along the way, God made their destination clear (Genesis 12:5). As we have noted, "they arrived there," and "there" would be the land of Canaan. This is it! They have made it through customs, had their passports stamped, and saw a big sign: "Welcome to Canaan: Future home of Abraham's descendants." Maybe it wasn't quite this way, but this was the long awaited earthly home God spoke to Abram about, and we find that alertness emerges as a pivotal step in the maze.

> Was not our father Abraham considered righteous for what he did when he offered his son Isaac on the altar? You see that his faith and his actions were working together, and his faith was made complete by what he did. And the scripture was fulfilled that says, "Abraham believed God, and it was credited to him as righteousness," and he was called God's friend. You see that a person is considered righteous by what they do and not by faith alone. (James 2:21–24)[4]

Upon entrance into Canaan, Abram would travel through the land on the ridge that runs north and south through the core of the country and is known as "the Ridge Route." Because we find the fathers of our faith, Abraham, Isaac, and Jacob, often walked this road, it is also known as "the Patriarchal Highway." On this highway, they would frequent towns like: Shechem, Bethel, Jerusalem, and Hebron. We will pass many of these cities as we hike with Abram on this "Patriarchal Highway" right into the heart of the Canaanite country. This is where we find Shechem is located and we meet up with Abram.

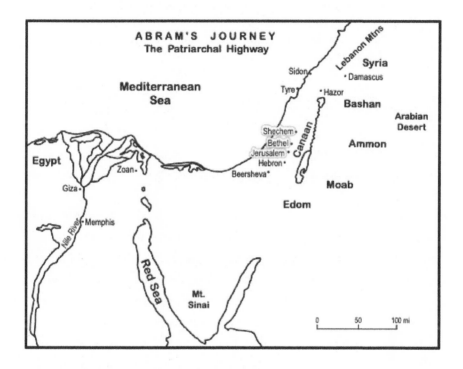

As he turns on "Alertness Avenue," Abram is vigilant to sense God's next step for him. Abram's watchful eye did not allow him to stop upon entry into the land, because God directed Abram and his crew to travel through the land until they arrived at the great tree of Moreh at Shechem. With confident faith in our God we will want to learn to attentively continue until we've reached the heart of God's will for us. In the very middle of this pagan, idol-worshiping country, Abram pauses to bow his knee before the true God who brought him to this point.

Again, the scholar, Bruce Waltke unpacks some valuable insights about Genesis 12:6a, *"Abram traveled through the land as far as the site of the great tree of Moreh at Shechem."*

> The Hebrew word for site means 'sacred site'. The mention
> of Shechem suggest it was an ancient sanctuary. This [great
> tree] is probably an oak tree whose greater height makes it a
> preferred place of worship (Genesis 13:18; 14:13; 18:1; 21:33).
> … Abraham's altar at this location may indicate his hope in
> God's promise of offspring and his hope that God will again
> speak to him. Although Abraham still worships according to
> the religious customs of his time, the content of his worship
> differs significantly.[5]

Now that Abram's faith was in the true God, he would use this as an opportunity to change the focus of the worship and begin a movement from false idol worship to worshipping the living God. Abram's alertness to God in worship impacted his descendants, a whole nation, and even us today.

This Step of Alertness demonstrates Abram's confident trust in his God. This is exactly how our lives need to mesh with Abram's in the maze. We can have courage to follow Jesus to the root of our issues, problems, and struggles but we may still experience fears and obstacles. Abram traveled hundreds of miles and worshiped the LORD fervently, but Sarai was still barren, and God's promise not yet fulfilled. We may be vigilant in worshiping Jesus and wholehearted in seeking Him only to still feel "barren" in our souls in regard to what God is doing in our lives. This is why alertness to what God is doing can be tricky. This is why we stay close to the LORD. This is why the Word of God enables us to hear the voice of God.

> How do you discern the voice of God? It starts with the Word of
> God. If you want to get a word *from* God, get into the Word of
> God. That's how you learn to discern the voice of God. After all
> it's the Spirit of God who inspired the Word of God. And when
> the Spirit of God quickens the Word of God, it's like hearing the
> voice of God in Dolby surround sound.[6]

Walking closely with Abram in the maze of life, we find that we deal with the same struggle of listening for the voice of God in the midst of our surroundings. With the Canaanites' worship of other gods, surely Abram was presented with the challenge of staying faithful to the true God. We see others in the maze, those who have taken different turns to pursue other gods, other priorities, and other plans. Regarding Sarai's infertility, Abram had a choice to trust the Canaanites' false gods of fertility or continue to confidently rely on the true life-giving God. When we face needs that seem to go unmet, we also have a choice to rely on the strength of our family and friends, on our own ingenuity, or confidently rely on the same God who supplies all our needs with His glorious riches, which have been given to us in Christ Jesus.[7]

Abram lived as a stranger in the land of Canaan, just as we who are believers are strangers on this earth. Like the farmer who heard the chirping of a cricket in New York City, as Christians we are not of this world and we must train our ears to listen for the voice of our King and our hearts for the promptings of the Spirit. The apostle Peter reminds us of our true identity in Christ and gives us these words of instruction and encouragement to live as strangers in this maze of life, just as Abram did.

> But you are not like that, for you are a chosen people. You are royal priests, a holy nation, God's very own possession. As a result, you can show others the goodness of God, for he called you out of the darkness into his wonderful light. "Once you had no identity as a people; now you are God's people. Once you received no mercy; now you have received God's mercy." Dear friends, I warn you as "temporary residents and foreigners" to keep away from worldly desires that wage war against your very souls. Be careful to live properly among your unbelieving neighbors. Then even if they accuse you of doing wrong, they will see your honorable behavior, and they will give honor to God when he judges the world. (1 Peter 2:9–12; NLT)

Not only do we take the Step of Alertness with confidence in our LORD, we look for confirmation from the LORD.

THE STEP OF ALERTNESS MEANS WE LOOK FOR THE CONFIRMATION OF THE LORD.

The LORD appeared to Abram and said, "To your offspring I will give this land."

Genesis 12:7a

We don't know exactly when was the last time the LORD spoke to him before Abram arrived in Canaan. Genesis 12:4–5 indicates that while in Haran the LORD gave Abram clear direction to go to Canaan. Perhaps these instructions came right as he left or a couple weeks before or even a year earlier, but nothing is said of the 350–400-mile trek from Haran to Canaan. It appears the LORD was amazingly silent during that journey. If we were traveling down the highway going about 60 miles per hour, that would mean that the Lord was silent for about six or seven hours. That would make for a long car ride. In Abram's day they walked, rode animals, and took wagons. They would travel approximately 20 miles in a day and with a caravan this large perhaps only 15 miles in a day. With a fairly consistent travel schedule, Abram and his travel companions would make this journey in about three to four weeks. We are not told if the LORD spoke to Abram during his month-long travel, but that would make for a very loud period of silence and very awkward, anxious steps. Perhaps this trip became more stressful as the group repeatedly asked, "Are we there yet?" It is not until Abram arrives in the middle of Canaanite country that we are informed *"The LORD appeared to Abram"* and there restates His promise.

> Wisdom consists of perceiving where God is going and then jumping on His bandwagon.
> **JAMES MONTGOMERY BOICE, COMMENTATOR**

As we follow the footsteps of Abram to the will of God, our friendship with Abram deepens, and we note that our stories are similar. The places are not all that different. The names then and the names now can be difficult to pronounce. The emotions can be like an avalanche crashing down on our minds. Our natural defaults of anger or lying or depression can kick in and overtake our thinking faster than we can imagine.

In the midst of all this, we want confirmation from the LORD. But what we find is that God does not give confirmation of His will until we step out in faith and do what we know God wants.

Several years ago, my wife and I found ourselves face-to-face with the question of God's will for our life in the maze. A church from Minneapolis and a church from Indianapolis both wanted me to candidate as their Youth Pastor. This choice of direction in the maze was extremely difficult for us. As we sought to be alert to the Lord, we felt a sense that we should pursue the church in Indianapolis, which meant we had to "burn the bridge" with the church in Minneapolis. The Indianapolis church voted with open arms for me to be their Youth Pastor. This was a confirmation from God. But my feeble mind wanted more from the Lord, and it began to creep into the area of hyper-alertness.

Once we accepted the position it would be a month before we would move and commence the ministry. During that month, I second-guessed myself, my wife, my Lord, and if I would have had one, my dog. I looked at everything that moved as though it would tell me again God's will and further confirm God's leading. It was a month of intense agony for me when it should have been a time of excited anticipation! I find it interesting that this was the same amount of time it took my friend Abram to travel from Haran to Canaan.

During this time I was working through Henry Blackaby's study *Experiencing God* where he said, "Our problem is that we pray and then never relate anything that happens to our praying."[8] My wife and I had sought the Lord and we felt confidence in His answer. So why did I not relate that answer to my prayer? God made known the next step for us in the maze and then He was silent, but I wanted more. God was silent because He had no new instructions for us. He had no other step until that one was taken. God would not fully confirm His will until we actually moved and began the ministry in Indianapolis. A statement I have found helpful in these painfully loud periods of silence is: "Far from being a sign of disapproval, seasons of silence may even be indicators of God's pleasure."[9]

We may experience deafening times of silence with the Lord, yet He directs as we move. As my good friend and Pastor of the church in Indianapolis Larry DeBruyn used to say, **"God always directs a moving object."** God has brought that saying to mind numerous times when trying to be alert to His will, and I have found myself telling others the saying as they seek to be vigilant in their footsteps to God's will.

Until we take the Step of Alertness and put feet to our faith, God will not give us the next step in the maze. Oh, by the way, those seven and a half years in Indianapolis were some of our best years in ministry with fond memories, good friends, and the birth of two of our children. Even if God had chosen to make those years difficult and unfruitful it would not change the fact that: "God always directs a moving object." Seeking God's confirmation leads us to communion with our LORD.

THE STEP OF ALERTNESS MEANS WE STAY IN COMMUNION WITH THE LORD.

> So he built an altar there to the LORD, who had appeared to him. From there he went on toward the hills east of Bethel and pitched his tent, with Bethel on the west and Ai on the east. There he built an altar to the LORD and called on the name of the LORD.
> **Genesis 12:7b–8**

We Commune with God by Putting Down Stakes, Genesis 12:7b.

Now that God had appeared to Abram and confirmed that this was the place, Abram demonstrates that he is beginning to put down his roots and leave his pre-Canaan days behind: *"So he (Abram) built an altar there to the LORD, who had appeared to him"* (Genesis 12:7b). Abram is "burning the bridge" to his old way of life and "building a bridge" to his new life in the land. This is what we might call a stake-in-the-ground moment.

Once again, my wife and I contemplated which way God wanted us to go in our maze as we encountered another ministry move. Similar to the previous account, we had two churches interested in my coming to be their Youth Pastor, one in Nebraska and one in Kansas City. This seems to be a trend; maybe God was preparing me for this book. I struggle with decision-making just like many of you, so God frequently brings me to these decision points in the maze to listen and be alert to Him. Each of us has areas of weakness that God navigates us into time and again to learn to rely on and commune with Him.

> ## Faith is like calories. You cannot see it but you can see its evidence.

This time both churches voted on the same night to have me come as their Youth Pastor and we wanted to be alert to God's leading. We only had 48 hours to decide. While contemplating our decision, we were involved in a Middle School Church Camp. As we prayed about what God wanted, the reasons to go to one of the churches began to emerge as the next turn to take in our lives' maze. Doubt, anxiety, and fear all played a role, but I remembered that at times like this to drive a mental stake in the ground at the place where you made the decision. Then when uncertainties come you can revisit that mental stake, and it will reassure you of God's leading. We drove a mental stake in a field at youth camp in Kansas, went home, and packed our bags for Nebraska. Abram did the same as he built an altar. He would return often to this altar and remember his commitment to be vigilant to God's leading.

We Commune with God by Building up Altars, Genesis 12:8a.

Building altars becomes a characteristic of his life and indicates Abram's continual longing to commune in worship with God by staying close to Him. Throughout Abram's life in Canaan, we see him habitually making an altar to worship, commune with, and seek the LORD. Throughout the remainder of his life, Abram will regularly return to these altars to be alert to what the LORD wants in his life. As we peruse Abram's time of communication with the LORD at the altar, we discover this was a way of life for him, and it should be for us as well. Let us notice the number of times it is mentioned that Abram built an altar and spent time with the LORD.

- Genesis 12:6–7; Abram **built an altar** at the great tree of Moreh at Shechem where the LORD appeared to him.

- Genesis 12:8; Abram **built an altar** between Bethel and Ai and called on the name of the LORD.

- Genesis 13:1–4; Abram **returned to the altar** he had built between Bethel and Ai and called on the name of the LORD.

- Genesis 13:18; Abram **built an altar** to the LORD near the trees of Mamre at Hebron.

- Genesis 14:18–20; Abram **worshiped the LORD** when he gave his tithe to Melchizedek the priest of God Most High.

- Genesis 15:1–21; Abram **worshiped the LORD** when a vision came to him for the Abrahamic Covenant.

- Genesis 17:3; Abram **worshiped the LORD** when the covenant of circumcision was instituted.

- Genesis 18:1–33; **The LORD appeared** to Abraham near the great trees of Mamre.

- Genesis 21:33; Abraham **planted a tamarisk tree** in Beersheba and **called upon the name of the LORD**, the Eternal God.

- Genesis 22:1–18; Abraham went to the region of Moriah to **worship the LORD** and sacrifice his son Isaac.

- From Genesis 13:18, we note the altar Abram built at Mamre and thus it implies his **lifestyle of worship.**

  » Genesis 23:1–2; Sarah died at Kiriath Arba, which is Hebron **which is Mamre.**

  » Genesis 23:17–20; Sarah was buried at Cave of Machpelah **near Mamre** which is Hebron.

  » Genesis 25:9–10; Abraham was buried at Cave of Machpelah **near Mamre** which is Hebron.

We Commune with God by Calling on His Name, Genesis 12:8b.

At these meeting times with God, Abram *"called on the name of the LORD"* (Genesis 12:8b). The names of God tell us about His nature, afford us the opportunity to better know Him, and help us to commune with Him. Let's look closer at three names of God that we find play an important role in the account of Abram.

- ➤ **LORD:** When the word lord is in all caps in the Old Testament it is God's personal name, Yahweh. It is like the first name, Bob or Nancy. This name is used in Exodus 3:14 when Moses asked God to identify Himself at the burning bush. God said, "I AM WHO I AM" which by "implication is that God's existence and character are determined by himself alone and are not dependent on anyone or anything else."[10] Genesis 12:8 is the first time the name LORD is used in Abram's story, and it signifies the personal intimacy that Abram now has with the living God.

- ➤ **The Eternal God:** "This name, 'the Most High God', emphasized God's strength, sovereignty, and supremacy."[11] Abram acknowledges and lives by the fact that God is the One True Most High God, which we have noted is a significant change in Abram's life from his early years. Abram first acknowledges this name when he gives tithes to the High Priest Melchizedek in Genesis 14:19. Abram expands our understanding of God as the Most High God by adding the descriptive phrase "Creator of heaven and earth." This signifies "God as the source of life, buoyancy, and joy in the trials of the day, not just as the source of origins."[12] Then, Abram calls on the name of the Most High God at Beersheba in Genesis 21:33.

> **The LORD Will Provide:** This comes from the often used Yahweh Yireh (also known as Jehovah Jireh) which means "the Lord sees and will provide." This is the description of God in Genesis 22:14 when the **Lord saw** that Abraham was willing to sacrifice Isaac; then the **Lord provided** a ram for the sacrifice. One commentator gives us this helpful insight: "The Lord sees the needs of those who come to worship him in his holy mount and is seen by them, that is, reveals himself to them by answering their prayers and providing their needs—his seeing takes practical effect in being seen."[13]

The reason it is significant for us to know our God is made clear by the prophet Daniel. He tells us that *"the people who know their God will display strength and take action"* (Daniel 11:32 NASB). We need to know who our God is so that we will be alert to what He wants and confidently rely on His strength to take the next step in our maze.

WATCH OBSERVANTLY IN THE MAZE

To take the Vigilant Step, we watch observantly for the Lord in the maze. We do this by training our feet to step in confidence with Him, our eyes to look for confirmation from Him, and our hearts to commune with Him. It is vital to our spiritual health to develop these steps of alertness if we want to commune with our Lord and stay in step with Him.

Rich Mullins and David Strasser (a.k.a. Beaker) wrote a tremendous song *Sometimes By Step*.[14] Allow the words to the second verse and chorus of the song to be a reminder of Abram's vigilance in his maze and to reinforce our alertness in our maze.

Sometimes I think of Abraham
How one star he saw had been lit for me
He was a stranger in this land
And I am that, no less than he
And on this road to righteousness
Sometimes the climb can be so steep
I may...

Oh God, You are my God
And I will ever praise You
Oh God, You are my God
And I will ever praise You
I will seek You in the morning
And I will learn to walk in Your ways
And step by step You'll lead me
And I will follow You all of my days.

The song touches on many areas we experience on our journey with Abram, but nothing epitomizes the step of vigilance like the words: *"I will seek You in the morning; And I will learn to walk in Your ways; And step by step You'll lead me; And I will follow You all of my days."* The challenge before us is to faithfully get to know our God, regularly seek our God, and continually learn to walk with our God.

At times we take this Step of Alertness to join God in what He is doing, and we have a sense of what God wants for our lives. At times we slip in taking the Step of Alertness, and we are not diligent to sense or act on God's will for us. This is when we need the next step: the Step of Faithfulness. Each of the steps we take, willingness, obedience, whole-heartedness, and alertness, needs to be accompanied alongside the Step of Faithfulness. Without the Step of Faithfulness, we will stumble when we take the other steps. So let's see what Abram has for us as we take "The Stick-to-itiveness Step."

MY VIGILANT STEP

THE VIGILANT STEP

➢ What are you vigilant about? What are you hypervigilant about?

➢ How is the call to follow Jesus the call to be "Vigilant?"

➢ How does Proverbs 20:24 help teach the Step of Alertness?

The LORD guides our steps, and we
never know where he will lead us.

PROVERBS 20:24 (ERV)

THE STEP OF ALERTNESS

**The Step of Alertness means
we go in the confidence of the LORD.**

➢ What did Abram do repeatedly that demonstrated his confidence
in his walk with the LORD? Why is this important to him and to us?

➤ When we accept Jesus as Savior, we are placed in Him. Peter gives us an amazing description of what it is like to be a Christian, or in Christ. From 1 Peter 2:9–12 below:

- Circle the descriptions of a Christian.
- Underline phrases or sentences that give us confidence in the Lord.

But you are a chosen people, a royal priesthood, a holy nation, God's special possession, that you may declare the praises of him who called you out of darkness into his wonderful light. Once you were not a people, but now you are the people of God; once you had not received mercy, but now you have received mercy. Dear friends, I urge you, as foreigners and exiles, to abstain from sinful desires, which wage war against your soul. Live such good lives among the pagans that, though they accuse you of doing wrong, they may see your good deeds and glorify God on the day he visits us.

1 PETER 2:9–12

- What do you want to remember from 1 Peter 2:9–12? Write it in a sentence here.

**The Step of Alertness means
we look for the confirmation of the LORD.**

➤ When does the LORD's confirmation usually come? What does God's silence mean? Is this difficult for you? Why or why not?

➤ Using Larry DeBruyn's statement, *"God always directs a moving object"* and the things we've learned from Abram, what are three statements you can make about the Step of Alertness in life's maze?

**The Step of Alertness means
we stay in communion with the LORD.**

---

*So he built an altar there to the LORD, who had
appeared to him. From there he went on toward the
hills east of Bethel and pitched his tent, with Bethel
on the west and Ai on the east. There he built an altar
to the LORD and called on the name of the LORD.*

GENESIS 12:7B–8

➢ We commune with God by putting down stakes. Genesis 12:7b

- How did Abram put down stakes?

- What "stake of commitment" do you need to drive in the
  ground right now? Why do you need to do that?

➤ We commune with God by building up altars. Genesis 12:8a

- Why is it important in the **Step of Alertness** that Abram continually built altars or returned to the altars he built?

- How do you need to build an altar of alertness right now? Or how do you need to return to an altar of alertness right now? What is it that is motivating you to go to the altar of God? What is keeping you from the altar of the LORD?

➤ We commune with God by calling on His name. Genesis 12:8b

- What does calling on the name of the LORD and doing God's will have to do with each other according to Daniel 11:32?

---

but the people who know their God will display strength and take action.

DANIEL 11:32 (NASB)

- Of the names of God associated with Abram's story, LORD, the Eternal God, the LORD will provide, which one do you need to call on right now? Why? How will you do that?

MY PERSONAL STEP OF ALERTNESS

➢ One specific thing I am dealing with when it comes to alertness is:

➢ In regard to the above, what is one step God wants me to take?

MY PRAYER OF ALERTNESS

➢ How do the lyrics to *Sometimes by Step* below help you understand **the Step of Alertness?**

> Oh God, You are my God
> And I will ever praise You
> I will seek You in the morning
> And I will learn to walk in Your ways
> And step by step You'll lead me
> And I will follow You all of my days

➢ Write below **a prayer of Alertness**. Use part or all of Mullins' song, if you'd like.

MY SAVIOR'S STEP OF ALERTNESS

*Then the Spirit led Jesus into the desert
to be tempted by the devil.*

MATTHEW 4:1 (NCV)

CHAPTER 5
THE STICK-TO-ITIVENESS STEP

AN UNSTOPPABLE WORD FOR THE MAZE

PETS ARE AS COMMON AS THE "COMMON COLD" AND COME IN AS MANY VARIETIES AS THE TYPES OF FLU. Individuals have dogs, cats, hamsters, snakes, fish, even alligators or pot belly pigs as pets. Many are cherished as family members, but few are as extraordinary as the Japanese Akita dog, Hachiko.[1]

In 1924, Hidesaburo Ueno, a professor at the Tokyo Imperial University, purchased Hachiko as his pet. At the end of each day, no matter whether it was a good day or a bad day, Ueno knew Hachiko would be faithfully waiting for his train to arrive at the station. In the heat, cold, rain, and snow, Hachiko would expectantly welcome his master home every day, until one day when Ueno did not arrive at the train station. He had died at work from a cerebral hemorrhage and would never come home to Hachiko again.

Ueno's death did not stop Hachiko's loyalty to his master. He continued daily to await Ueno's arrival at the train station, but he never came. Individuals would try to coax the dog away from the train station and even adopt him, but nothing or no one would deter Hachiko from his daily mission to wait for his master. Until his death nearly ten years later, each and every day Hachiko could be found at the train station anxiously awaiting his master's return. Hachiko's life exemplified what it means to be faithful and loyal.

Hachiko's remarkable story of faithfulness pales when placed next to the incomprehensible faithfulness of our God. A God whose promises are as good as done and His faithfulness can be compared to the consistency of the rising of the sun: *"Because of the Lord's great love we are not consumed, for his compassions never fail.* ***They are new every morning; great is your faithfulness"*** (Lamentations 3:22–23).

Following Abram's footsteps to the will of God we find *The Stick-to-itiveness Step,* which is also known as *the Step of Faithfulness.* Stick-to-itiveness is defined as, "dogged perseverance: tenacity."[2] But of course we will check the **BADEW**[3] to find out that Stick-to-itiveness means: "to hang in there; endure difficulties; stubbornness; tirelessness; stick like gum on the bottom of a shoe."

In 1 Corinthians 4:2 (NET), we note that the apostle Paul draws attention to the fact that faithfulness is a valued and needed quality for marking out a path to God's will in the maze; *"Now what is sought in stewards is that one be found **faithful**."* The fruit of the Spirit is an essential character quality for a traveler in the maze. One of the aspects of the fruit of the Spirit is faithfulness: *"But the fruit of the Spirit is love, joy, peace, patience, kindness, goodness, **faithfulness**, gentleness, and self-control"* (Galatians 5:22–23a). Upon completion of our time in the maze of this life, it is our desire to hear Jesus say these words to us: *"Well done, good and faithful servant; you have been faithful over a few things; I will make you ruler over many things. Enter into the joy of your lord"* (Matthew 25:21, 23).

With these foundational comments on faithfulness in mind, we once again accompany Abram in life's maze. We find his life is an example of faithfulness, and Abram models for us three important facets of the meaning of faithfulness as we take "The Stick-to-itiveness Step." This Step of Faithfulness means we will give priority to our relationship with God; we will face tests in our relationship with God; and we will respond to our relationship with God.

My steps have held to your paths;
my feet have not slipped.
Psalm 17:5

TAKE THE STEP OF FAITHFULNESS IN THE MAZE

From there he went on toward the hills east of Bethel and pitched his tent, with Bethel on the west and Ai on the east. There he built an altar to the LORD and called on the name of the LORD. Then Abram set out and continued toward the Negev.
Genesis 12:8–9

THE STEP OF FAITHFULNESS MEANS WE GIVE PRIORITY TO OUR RELATIONSHIP WITH GOD. GENESIS 12:8

From there he went on toward the hills east of Bethel and pitched his tent, with Bethel on the west and Ai on the east. There he built an altar to the LORD and called on the name of the LORD.
Genesis 12:8

In taking *The Vigilant Step* we realize the importance of being alert in our walk with the LORD. Now Abram takes us to another level in our relationship with God by *The Stick-to-itiveness Step*. Abram's example is not only to spend time with our God but to faithfully make our relationship with God a priority. As we navigate our lives' maze, we will make wrong turns, find ourselves at dead ends, and at times take steps backwards. But remember God always directs a moving object. It has been said "The Christian life is a direction not perfection," and it would be good for us to keep this statement at the forefront of our thoughts as we trod on earth's sod. Yes, there are times to stop, evaluate, and seek God, but we are not to camp in one area longer than God wants. We desire our time in the maze to be characterized by our faithfulness to God.

"Put first things first."[4] This is a very simple definition of a priority and a root of faithfulness, yet an extremely difficult action to consistently execute. As Abram settles in the rugged terrain between Bethel and Ai, his priority is clear. Abram put first things first when he took the needed time to build an altar to the LORD so he could faithfully commune with his God. Our ultimate priority also is to be faithful in our getting to know and follow our Lord Jesus Christ.

> The glory of God's faithfulness is that no sin of ours has ever made Him unfaithful.
> ### CHARLES SPURGEON, PREACHER

When I was a Youth Pastor, one day I came into my office to find a baby food jar containing a walnut and rice sitting on my desk. This was not a common occurrence, so naturally my curiosity was piqued. Though I never knew who left that jar on my desk, I have not forgotten the lesson it taught me. I found a note that explained the meaning of the walnut and rice in the jar. Our lives are like putting a walnut in a baby food jar and filling the rest with rice. If I put Jesus in first, He fits. The rest of the things in my life will fall into place. However, if I put the rice in first and then try to fit in the walnut, it will not fit; at least, not without some major rearrangement. The point is simple and profound! If I allow or put "rice" in my life first, then it will be next to impossible to squeeze Jesus into my life, especially at the center of my life. This is why Jesus instructs us to put him in our lives first making Him the main thing. Jesus was straightforward when He told us, *"But seek first his kingdom and his righteousness, and all these things will be given to you as well"* (Matthew 6:33).

We develop the faithfulness God desires in our lives as we are devoted to seeking Him first.

At this point in the maze, we relate to Abram in his decision and struggle to faithfully put God first. Abram was right in the middle of a heathen Canaanite culture that did not worship or place value on Abram's God. We face the adversity of a culture that has moved into the status of "anti-Christian." Abram's visible altar would not be easy to build, he would possibly find opposition, and he probably had to face some of his "old idols." The busyness and clutter of our culture does not make it easy to build an intimate relationship with Jesus and makes it easy for us to pursue other "idols." Making decisions to do things God's way and to allow His will to be done in our lives will bring misunderstanding and opposition. We must confront anything or anyone that we tend to put in the jar ahead of Jesus. These "old" priorities will always fight to be the main thing, but we must keep the main thing the main thing. Allowing Jesus the preeminence in our lives is the main thing! Priorities are hard because they are visible, keep us accountable, and cause us to face tough issues in our lives. But that is when we find out if we are faithfully making our relationship with Jesus the first thing and putting the first thing, first.

THE STEP OF FAITHFULNESS MEANS WE FACE TESTS IN OUR RELATIONSHIP WITH GOD. GENESIS 12:8

As we see our friend Abram settling into his new land and phase of life, there are a number of tests that he will encounter which threaten his faithfulness to the LORD. Commentator Bruce Waltke captures a picture of the various tests of trials Abram faced during his journey through his maze and presents them as though we are looking through a photo album of Abram's faithfulness.

> The plot is driven by Abraham's struggle to trust God in the face of a series of conflicts testing his faith. His faith develops as he trusts God in spite of a childless wife, famine in the Promised

Land, exile in a hostile land, the kidnapping of his wife in pagan kings' harems, an ungrateful nephew who seizes land for himself, war against mighty kings, family strife between rival wives and their children, his withering body, and death itself with the promise unfulfilled. In addition, Abraham's God is mysterious, asking Abraham to sacrifice the child in whom his offspring will be reckoned.[5]

Yes, the account of Abram's life reveals his flaws, but in the midst of them he is put in the crucible of trials and emerges as a great example of faithfulness. In Genesis 12:8, we watch as Abram takes a stand to worship the one true living God in the neighborhood of polytheistic, dead, idol worshipers. Abram might have struggled with his natural tendency to lie in this difficult situation, but we see his amazing transformation of trust during the pinnacle of his tests. The climax is seen when Abram willingly offers his son as a sacrifice on Mt. Moriah and passes the test of faithfulness with an A.

Abram's character of faithfulness is so strong that when the crucial moment of slaying his son came, Abram thought God would bring his son back from the dead.

> By faith Abraham, when God tested him, offered Isaac as a sacrifice. He who had embraced the promises was about to sacrifice his one and only son, even though God had said to him, "It is through Isaac that your offspring will be reckoned." Abraham reasoned that God could even raise the dead, and so in a manner of speaking he did receive Isaac back from death. (Hebrews 11:17–19)

At this call to go and sacrifice his son Isaac, through whom a great nation was promised, Abram got up early, cut the wood for the sacrifice, called his servant, took Isaac, and headed for a monumental act of obedience and faithfulness.[6] Our tendency might have been to sleep in, drag our feet, and try to negotiate with God. In Genesis 22, Abram's willingness to offer Isaac demonstrates the maturity of Abram's faithfulness; however, here in Genesis 12 we note the infant steps of Abram's faithfulness as he continually took time to worship, seek, and become intimate with his God.

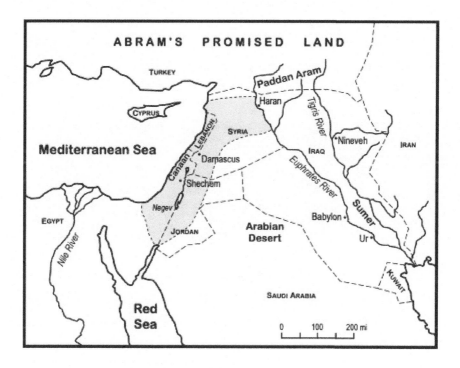

Abram's faithfulness to the LORD continued to be put to the test throughout his time in the earthly maze. As he hiked throughout the land, Abram longed for the fulfillment of God's promise to give him the land, to make a great nation from his descendants, and to dwell in a city that God built. But at the time of his death, Abram only owned the field and cave he purchased to bury his wife Sarai.[7] He did not possess the land God promised. He died having seen Isaac marry Rebekah and a few grandchildren but not the great and mighty nation God promised. Abram would not find the city whose architect and builder was God on this earth. From the map, it can be seen that at his death, the land promised Abram would still be future, yet in pursuing God's will Abram proved himself faithful.

With this in mind, we must make note of the amazing commentary on Abram and Sarai (as well as all the men and women of faith) given by the writer of the book of Hebrews. *"These were all commended for their faith, **yet none of them received what had been promised,** since God had planned something better for us so that only together with us would they be made perfect"* (Hebrews 11:39–40). "None of them received what had been promised!" I read this passage many times before I realized that the men and women of faith had not received their promise this side of heaven.

> The goal of faithfulness is not that we will do work for God, but that he will be free to do His work through us.... God wants to use us as He used His own Son.
>
> ### OSWALD CHAMBERS, AUTHOR

Abram and Sarai were faithful to carry out their parts during their time in the maze, and now we have a great responsibility to be faithful to our part and join the men and women of faith. God's character of faithfulness gives us assurance that God will carry out His part in His time and in His way. God will not fail to keep His promise because the Scripture is clear, and we have confidence in life's challenges that *"God is not a man, so he does not lie. He is not human, so he does not change his mind. Has he ever spoken and failed to act? Has he ever promised and not carried it through?"* (Numbers 23:19).

As we seek to comprehend how the men and women of faith work together to accomplish God's will, consider the story of the ant and the contact lens. Brenda and her friends decided to go rock climbing. As they were scaling the massive rock, about half way up they paused on a ledge. As they took the breather, Brenda's safety rope snapped against her eye knocking out one of her contact lens. Hundreds of feet from the ground and hundreds of feet from the top of the rock, Brenda frantically searched with no success for her contact lens. Blurry-eyed, frustrated, and upset, Brenda and her friends started climbing again. She prayed, "Lord, You can see all things without contacts. You know every stone, leaf, and stick on this cliff, and You know exactly where my contact lens is. Please help me." The group of climbers finally made it to the top and then walked down the trail to the bottom of the rock. A new party of climbers was set to attack the face of the cliff when one of them shouted, "Hey, anybody lose a contact lens?" Flabbergasted, Brenda asked, "How did you find my contact?" One of the climbers explained that he saw an ant slowly moving across the face of the rock carrying it. Brenda told her father who was a cartoonist. He drew a picture of an ant lugging a huge contact lens with the caption, "Lord, I don't know why You want me to carry this thing. I can't eat it, it does me no good, and its heavy, but if this is what You want me to do, I'll carry it for You."

We find some connections between this story and our faithfulness in the maze. First, we may not know why we are carrying something heavy in life, but the Lord knows. Second, we may not know what God is doing behind the scenes, but He does. Third, we may not know who has gone before us so that together we complete God's work and accomplish God's will, but the Lord does. In Romans 4, God gives us another glimpse of how Abram's faithfulness and ours work together to reflect God's character.

> Abraham never wavered in believing God's promise. In fact, his faith grew stronger, and in this he brought glory to God. He was fully convinced that God is able to do whatever he promises. And because of Abraham's faith, God counted him as righteous. And when God counted him as righteous, it wasn't just for Abraham's benefit. It was recorded for our benefit, too, assuring us that God will also count us as righteous if we believe in him, the one who raised Jesus our Lord from the dead. (Romans 4:20–24 NLT)

THE STEP OF FAITHFULNESS MEANS WE RESPOND IN OUR RELATIONSHIP WITH GOD. GENESIS 12:9

Then Abram set out and continued toward the Negev.
Genesis 12:9

It is easy to read over this little verse without much consideration, but it adds much to our understanding of navigating life's maze. Abram continues his travels from the hill country of Bethel and Ai south along the Parochial Highway to the Negev. The Negev is a desert area. It is a hot, barren area where Abram would continue his journey with the LORD. Later in Abram's account, we will find him again in the Negev, this time at Beersheba. We observe three principles from Abram's move to the Negev.

When we faithfully respond to the Lord, we will walk in our uncomfortable zones.

Abram went to the Negev. While there he experienced a severe famine and headed to Egypt for relief (Genesis 12:9–10). When we talk about getting out of our "comfort zones," we are really saying we will be in our "uncomfortable zones." Walking in our uncomfortable zones is where our faithfulness is proved to be genuine.

When we get serious about following God in our life's maze, He always leads us into uncomfortable waters where the waves are just above our nose of comfort. It reminds me of the time I was a youngster at summer camp. I was not a very good swimmer and found myself in an area of the pool where the water was just over my nose. I was bouncing up and down to try and get my breath and to keep from what I thought would have been a watery death. If my timing was off, I would take a deep breath of pool water. The little waves of water would crash on my face, blinding me to the edge of the pool which was just barely out of my reach. Thinking that I was going to see Jesus, I finally pushed myself, reached out, grabbed the side of the pool, and pulled myself to safety. This seems to be my experience of walking with God through the uncomfortable zones in the maze. God always asks me to be in water just a bit over my nose and level of comfort. He asks me to be faithful to His call and trust Him to get me safely to where I need to be.

As we swim in water that is just over our noses, we learn four lessons about our uncomfortable zones. First, our uncomfortable zone is demanding. Generally, the sun beat down on the Negev. Water, food, and supplies were at a premium. Most of the Negev was not for the faint of heart. God may have us walk in the uncomfortable arena of physical ailments or difficult relationships.

Genesis 12:10 tells us of three more uncomfortable zones: *"Now there was a famine in the land, and Abram went down to Egypt to live there for a while because the famine was severe."* The second lesson we learn is that our uncomfortable zone is daunting. Abram experienced a time of very little to no food. He probably experienced some anxious, sleepless nights as he felt responsible for Sarai, his livestock, and his workers. Many times we stare into the dark eyes of our fears when our needs and sometimes wants are threatened or unmet.

Third, our uncomfortable zone is distressing. When Abram went to Egypt, he faced another unfamiliar country and culture. Abram may have been tempted by the gods of the Egyptians, especially because of the famine. We know he gave in to the temptation to lie about his wife to Pharaoh. The uncomfortable zone may emerge at our places of employment, school, community, or even at home, when those around us do not hold to the same biblical values we do. We may be in an area where we come face to face with our sinful tendencies in the uncomfortable waters of life.

It could almost go unsaid but needs to be stated. Fourth, our uncomfortable zone is difficult. *"The famine was severe"* (Genesis 12:10b). Not only did Abram's clan face a famine, the writer of Genesis wanted us to know it was a bad one. The uncomfortable zone is never slightly uncomfortable, it is REALLY uncomfortable. Paul Tournier puts into words what most of us think, but he also confronts us with the truth:

> We are nearly always longing for an easy religion, easy to
> understand and easy to follow; a religion with no mystery, no
> insoluble problems, no snags; a religion that would allow us to
> escape from our miserable human condition; a religion in which
> contact with God spares us all strife, all uncertainty, all suffering
> and all doubt; in short, a religion without the Cross.[8]

Our tendency is to avoid these difficult, uncomfortable waters and ask for smooth, comfortable water, but the uncomfortable zone is unavoidable and needful in moving us through the maze of life.

When we faithfully respond to the Lord, we will walk in the way of wisdom.

During the writing of this book, I ventured down a very precarious alley in the maze of my life. My Dad was on Home Hospice Care, but it had become evident that now it was time to move him to the Hospice House. I went to talk with my Mom who was coming down the hall. Her face drooped, her speech slurred, and her mental faculties were disoriented. While the Hospice worker was there for my Dad, we called 911 for my Mom. All of a sudden, decisions began to come at me in rapid fire succession. With the first responders there to deal with my Mom's medical condition, and the Hospice individuals there to deal with my Dad's ailing condition, I was forced to make some quick and critical decisions. I did not have the privilege of calling for a prayer meeting or contacting the church's prayer chain to seek God's will because the paramedic was looking me square in the eye to make a split second decision on my mom's medical condition. I am grateful to the Lord that both of their needs were taken care of in that moment of crisis. My Mom received the medical attention she needed at the local hospital, and my Dad passed away quietly in his sleep at the Hospice House.

> The nearer to heaven
> the steeper the mountains.
> **W.H. GRIFFITH THOMAS[9]**

This is where the Step of Faithfulness becomes a giant one in the maze. God gives us a mind to think, wisdom from Him, and principles from His Scriptures to guide our decisions. As we continue to walk in faithfulness with the Lord, a by-product is making wise, godly decisions. So, do we pray about the kind of toothpaste to buy? Going to the lake with friends? Which car to buy? Whom to marry? Which job to take? This is where we take the principles of God's Word and the wisdom He has given us to walk willingly in His way. We grow in wisdom through life's experiences and through the word of God. Yes, there are many times we will sense a need to pray, and so that's what we do. Never minimize the power and place of prayer for God's will to be done. Also, never minimize the need to faithfully walk with the Lord as Abram did by setting out and continuing toward the Negev. So as we faithfully walk with the Lord, we too will choose the way of wisdom and not come to God only in times of need.

When we faithfully respond to the Lord, we will walk in the character of God.

God is continually behind the scenes changing the set, providing new props, and bringing new cast members onto the stage of our lives. God changed Abram's set from the Negev to Egypt. He provided a twist in the plot by having Abram face a famine. God also brought the Pharaoh on the scene to have Abram deal with his propensity to lie. As we follow the footsteps of Abram to the will of God, always remember that God is at work through the good, the bad, and the ugly times.

In my early twenties, I experienced what I thought was a bad time; however, I learned a painfully freeing lesson about how God's will works and how God works to make me like Jesus Christ at each turn in the maze. Naturally, this lesson involved a girl I was interested in; okay really interested in. And of course, she was not interested in me, but unlike the movies I did not get the girl in the end.

I began to think about this "non-romantic" relationship in regard to Romans 8:28 which says, *"And we know that **in all things God works** for the good of those who love him, who have been called according to his purpose."* What I have come to understand is that "all things" include: our relationships, our non-relationships, our disappointments, our achievements, our struggles, our joys, our heartaches, our hopes, our sin (remember the story of Monessa), and of course everything else. All means all!

God did not stop at verse 28, and neither should we. The next verse, Romans 8:29, has many big theological words and has spawned much debate, but I don't want us to miss the reason God uses everything in our lives: *"For those God foreknew he also predestined **to be conformed to the image of his Son**, that he might be the firstborn among many brothers and sisters."* God's purpose in life is to use everything to mold us and shape our lives to be like Jesus Christ. If we make the wrong turn in the maze, or we wander down the wrong path for years, or we make the right choice, or we stand still, God will use it to make us more like Jesus! God is continually about His business of accomplishing His will in spite of us, not because of us.

This is not to say it doesn't matter how we follow Jesus or that our choices do not matter. What matters is that Jesus is seen more and more in our lives as we walk the path through the maze of life. There is a freedom in walking in faithfulness. There is a comfort in our mistakes, our blunders, our sins, our successes, our victories, our joys that God is right there using them to make us more like Jesus and guide us to take a step towards His will. Through our faithfulness in the maze, Christ's character is being developed more and more. Remember, God is not hiding His will from us, and He wants us to know it more than we do.

There is hope for us in who Jesus is and what He does. Sometimes, He gets us where God wants us by disappointment or heartache, but He is working all things to His good and using it to make us into His image. Oh, by the way, the next girl in my life didn't break my heart; she captured my heart! She is my wife, and we have been navigating the maze of life together for over thirty years.

A little thing is a little thing, but faithfulness in the little things is a great thing.

HUDSON TAYLOR, MISSIONARY

KEEP PLUGGING IN THE MAZE

The application for us is simple yet hard: keep plugging away in our life's maze. We keep on keeping on by focusing on the very characteristic of God He is developing in us—faithfulness. God's faithfulness is evident throughout the Scriptures, but let us ponder a few passages in the Psalms. Remember, the psalmists climbed the same rocky terrain of life's maze we do, so let their description of God's faithfulness soak in until it penetrates the fiber of our souls, and we become men and women of faithfulness.

- Psalm 36:5, "Your love, O LORD, reaches to the heavens, **your faithfulness to the skies.** Your righteousness is like the mighty mountains, your justice like the great deep."

- Psalm 86:15, "But you, O Lord, are a compassionate and gracious God, slow to anger, **abounding in love and faithfulness.**"

- Psalm 115:1, "Not to us, O LORD, not to us but to your name be the glory, **because of your love and faithfulness.**"

- Psalm 117:2, "For great is his love toward us, and **the faithfulness of the LORD endures forever.**"

- Psalm 119:90, "**Your faithfulness continues through all generations;** you established the earth and it endures."

- Psalm 138:2, "I will bow down toward your holy temple and **will praise your name for your love and your faithfulness,** for you have exalted above all things your name and your word."

Psalm 145:13, "Your kingdom is an everlasting kingdom, and your dominion endures through all generations. **The LORD is faithful to all his promises** and loving toward all he has made."

- Psalm 146:6, "the Maker of heaven and earth, the sea, and everything in them – **the LORD who remains faithful forever.**"

By focusing on our heavenly Father's great faithfulness, we are changed. We begin to take on the family resemblance as we realize "that the highest reward for a faithful life is not what you get for it but what you become by it."[10] Then we can join with Thomas Chisholm who penned that the great old hymn, **"Great Is Thy Faithfulness."**[11]

Great Is Thy faithfulness, O God my Father!
There is no shadow of turning with Thee;
Thou changest not, Thy compassions, they fail not
As Thou hast been Thou forever wilt be.

Chorus:
Great Is Thy faithfulness,
Great Is Thy faithfulness,
Morning by morning new mercies I see;
All I have needed Thy hand hath provided
Great is Thy Faithfulness, Lord unto me!

The Step of Faithfulness is the call to be devoted to the faithful One throughout all of our days in the maze. God will faithfully meet us at the point of our need, just as He did with Abram, Sarai, and all the men and women of faith who have walked before us. Not only do we take the Step of Faithfulness, we take the steps of willingness, obedience, wholeheartedness, and alertness. Wherever we are in the maze we must take the next step, but it begins by taking a baby step.

MY STICK-TO-ITIVENESS STEP

THE STICK-TO-ITIVENESS STEP

➤ What are some examples of faithfulness and/or unfaithfulness in our culture?

➤ How is the call to follow Jesus like having "Stick-to-itiveness?"

➢ How does Psalm 17:5 help teach the Step of Faithfulness?

My steps have held to your paths;
my feet have not slipped.

PSALM 17:5

THE STEP OF FAITHFULNESS

**The Step of Faithfulness means we will
give priority to our relationship with God.**

➤ Write below. Explain to a friend, the story of the walnut in the jar and how that illustrates giving priority to your relationship with God.

➤ Currently, my relationship with Jesus Christ is:

- ❑ A priority in my life
- ❑ Squeezed out by rice (something else)
- ❑ Weak from battling the cares of this life
- ❑ Barely a relationship
- ❑ Other:

➤ Right now, what is one thing God wants you to do to keep your relationship with Him the main thing?

**The Step of Faithfulness means
we will face tests in our relationship with God.**

➤ Which of the trials of Abram can you relate to (check all
that apply):

- ❐ Childless – the trial of pain
- ❐ Famine – the trial of unmet needs
- ❐ Kidnapping of wife – the trial of anxiety
- ❐ Ungrateful and greedy family – the trial of being abused
- ❐ War with Kings – the trial of work stress
- ❐ Family strife over decisions – the trial of regret
- ❐ Withering body – the trial of an aging or ailing body
- ❐ Death – the trial of grief
- ❐ Other –
- ❐ Other –

➤ What are three observations you can make from Hebrews 11:39–40
about the Abram, faithfulness, and us?

---

*These were all commended for their faith, yet none
of them received what had been promised, since
God had planned something better for us so that
only together with us would they be made perfect.*
HEBREWS 11:39–40

➤ Whatever God is asking you to do right now, how can the Step of Faithfulness be a part of it?

The Step of Faithfulness means we will respond in our relationship with God.

So he built an altar there to the LORD, who had appeared to him. From there he went on toward the hills east of Bethel and pitched his tent, with Bethel on the west and Ai on the east. There he built an altar to the LORD and called on the name of the LORD. Then Abram set out and continued toward the Negev.

GENESIS 12:7B–9

➤ When we faithfully respond to the LORD, we will walk in our uncomfortable zones.

- As Abram faithfully followed the LORD, what uncomfortable zones did God ask him to walk in?

- For you to be faithful in your next step with the LORD, what uncomfortable zone(s) is God asking you to walk in?

➢ When we faithfully respond to the LORD, we will walk in the way of wisdom.

- How would you describe the way of wisdom as it relates to God's will?

- What wisdom has God already given you for the decision facing you in your life's maze?

➢ When we faithfully respond to the LORD, we will walk in the character of our God.

*And we know that in **all things God works** for the good of those who love him, who have been called according to his purpose. For those God foreknew he also predestined **to be conformed to the image of his Son**, that he might be the firstborn among many brothers and sisters.*

ROMANS 8:28–29

- What does Romans 8:28–29 teach you about God's faithfulness?

- How does the discussion of Romans 8:28–29 impact your thinking about God's will?

MY PERSONAL STEP
OF FAITHFULNESS

➢ Which of the Psalms, from pages 133-134, about God's faithfulness ministers to you? Write it below in your own words.

➢ When it comes to faithfulness, God wants me to:

MY PRAYER OF FAITHFULNESS

➤ Take time to think about the words and/or sing Thomas Chisholm's great old hymn **"Great Is Thy Faithfulness."**

> Great Is Thy faithfulness, O God my Father!
> There is no shadow of turning with Thee;
> Thou changest not, Thy compassions, they fail not
> As Thou hast been Thou forever wilt be.
>
> Chorus:
> Great Is Thy faithfulness,
> Great Is Thy faithfulness,
> Morning by morning new mercies I see;
> All I have needed Thy hand hath provided
> Great is Thy Faithfulness, Lord unto me!

➤ Write *a prayer of faithfulness below*, and then spend time praying it to the LORD.

MY SAVIOR'S STEP
OF FAITHFULNESS

Faithful is He (Jesus) who calls you,
and He also will bring it to pass.

1 THESSALONIANS 5:24 (NASB)

SUMMARY
THE
BABY
STEP

OUT OF THE MAZE
WITH BABY STEPS

WHAT ABOUT BOB? IS ONE of my all-time favorite movies. Bob Wylie, played by Bill Murray, is a man who describes himself as having "problems." He is plagued by a number of mental health issues, including OCD—obsessive-compulsive disorder, anxiety, and depression. Bob has gone from therapist to therapist seeking relief from his maladies, but his problems have only worsened. Finally, he goes for help to Dr. Leo Marvin, played by Richard Dreyfuss. Dr. Marvin has developed a new "breakthrough" psychotherapy treatment called "Baby Steps." Dr. Marvin has also written a book by the same name. He suggests that Bob read it and incorporate the techniques.

The premise of "Baby Steps" is to break your problems into small baby steps which are achievable and manageable instead of looking at the largeness and severity of your issues. As Dr. Marvin explains this concept to Bob, he starts to put the principle into action by walking around the doctor's office repeating the words, "Baby Steps." Bob is off to a good start as he takes baby steps around Dr. Marvin's office, down the hall, and onto the elevator. However, when the elevator begins its descent, one can hear Bob let out a loud scream of terror.

We are like Bob in that we take "Baby Steps" throughout the maze of our lives until one day God has us exit the maze. At times the steps are exciting. At times the steps are scary. But we must realize and remember that we navigate the maze of life one step at a time. We will not get through the maze without running into walls. We will not get through the maze without making wrong turns. We will find ourselves going the wrong way at times. Let us take each of the five steps that Abram has shown us and break them into baby steps so that as we move through the maze of life we will become more and more like Jesus Christ.

Your way went through the sea and
Your path through the great waters,
but Your footprints were unseen.
Psalm 77:19 (HCSB)

OUT OF THE MAZE
WITH A COMPASS

Each of the principles we have examined is a compass to guide us in the direction God would have us go. They are not a "formula" to "magically" transport us to the destination called "God's Will." So, we diligently watch for the opportunities to use each one of the compasses and carefully examine how it points us to the Lord and His way. Then, it is necessary to apply the principle. In one sector of the maze, we might reach into our knapsack and pull out the principle of whole-heartedness, followed by willingness, and then faithfulness. Another area of the maze requires us to use the principle of alertness, which leads us to obedience. Because of our tendency to veer off course, and even stand still, we keep each of the principles ready to use and reuse at a moment's notice to check our steps and direct our course.

As each compass is used it will point towards the Lord. Then it is necessary for us to take a baby step in that direction. We may need to pull out the compass of willingness time and again in the maze as we continually face a new turn. The deeper we travel in the maze the more indispensable the compass of obedience is as we face daily twists. As God causes us to explore the outlining areas of our heart, the compass of wholeheartedness reveals we have drifted into half-heartedness. The compass of alertness points out sections of our lives where we have become dull in sensing the Lord's leading. The compass of faithfulness reveals that our choices have now put us on the path of unfaithfulness in the journey. If charted, our pilgrimage would look a lot like the stock market with many ups and downs. Sometimes the ups are way up, and sometimes the downs are way down, but the goal is to move toward the exit of the maze with a growing Christlikeness. Further reflection on each compass will assist us in applying the needed principle.

> When God is in it...it flows.
> When the flesh is in it... it is forced.
> **CHARLES SWINDOLL, AUTHOR**

Is God wanting us to take the Step of Willingness? Then God wants us to travel lightly in the maze. Our will is to be as neutral as it can be to allow Jesus to dictate the next step. The baby Step of Willingness can be the trickiest because we are dealing with motives, but with it we are moving in the direction God wants us to go. Releasing our wills to the Lord, not carrying excess baggage, and concentrating on Jesus enable us to travel lightly in the maze so God can easily direct us.

Is God wanting us to take the Step of Obedience? Then God wants us to love deeply in the maze. The way we tell Jesus we love Him is to obey His Word. When you have a clear sense of what He wants you to do, then do it without hesitation. Let your relationship with Jesus become the deepest and strongest love in your life. This is a tough step because obedience is a "rubber meets the road" step. Jesus says, *"If you really love Me, I will put you in a position where you will need to take a baby Step of Obedience to demonstrate your love for Me."*

Is God wanting us to take the Step of Wholeheartedness? Then God wants us to proclaim it loudly in the maze. In this step we will not hold back anything from the Lord and our stand for Him will make a loud proclamation that Jesus is on the throne of every area of our hearts. Sometimes others will notice our wholehearted allegiance to the Lord, and that will speak volumes, other times it may be a small area of our hearts that we finally give to the Lord, but it proclaims to Jesus that He has our inner most being. Our baby step into wholeheartedness is needed in the maze of life.

Is God wanting us to take the Step of Alertness? Then God wants us to watch observantly in the maze. Keep close in your relationship with God and keep it alive. At times a baby Step of Obedience will become clear from God's Word and our relationship with Him. Develop a sensitivity to the things of the Lord, and remember the words of the Apostle Paul, *"Since, then, you have been raised with Christ, set your hearts on things above, where Christ is seated at the right hand of God"* (Colossians 3:1).

Is God wanting us to take the Step of Faithfulness? Then God wants us to walk consistently in the maze. Faithfulness is such a vital step in our journey through the maze of life. It means we are continually seeking to take baby steps in the right direction even when we make a wrong or sinful step. God rewards faithfulness, and it infiltrates each of the other steps.

OUT OF THE MAZE WITH A FRIEND

One of the most amazing compliments in the entire Bible is given to Abram. Three times we are told that **Abram is "God's friend"** (2 Chronicles 20:7; Isaiah 41:8; James 2:23). Through our time with Abram in life's maze we have become Abram's friend and through Abram we too have become God's friend. As we leave our time in the maze with Abram, we pause to look at the benefit of this unbelievable friendship. Nestled in the passage we have examined are the details of the Abrahamic covenant of which we jumped over, until now. This remarkable covenant is chronicled for us in Genesis 12:2–3.

> "I will make you into a great nation,
> and I will bless you;
> I will make your name great,
> and you will be a blessing.
> I will bless those who bless you,
> and whoever curses you I will curse;
> and all peoples on earth
> will be blessed through you."

We want to note God's threefold promise: (1) Abram would be a great nation; (2) Abram would have a great name; (3) through Abram all the peoples on the earth will be blessed. The Apostle Paul expanded this third promise to us when he said:

> Know then that it is those of faith who are the sons of Abraham. And the Scripture, foreseeing that God would justify the Gentiles by faith, preached the gospel beforehand to Abraham, saying, 'in you shall all the nations be blessed.' So then, those who are of faith are blessed along with Abraham, the man of faith. Galatians 3:7–9 (ESV)

We are blessed because God chose to send the Savior of the world, Jesus Christ, through the Abram's descendants.

> By embracing the faith of Abraham, mankind would be reconciled to God. The separation sin created could be bridged after all, but not through any scheme created by man—only by the grace of God. With Abraham, the story of reconciliation began. It's a story of forgiveness and redemption—a story that would continue for hundreds of years. **A story that would eventually become your story and mine.**[1] (emphasis added)

We can see Abram's story and our story interlocked at every step along the way. What was a baby Step of **Willingness** Abram took? He gave up his idols to follow the true and living God, and so we put Jesus in the place only He deserves in our lives. What was a baby Step of **Obedience** Abram took? He left his homeland to go to the land God promised him. We do what God asks us to do according to His Word. What was a baby Step of **Wholeheartedness** Abram took? He took everything God asked him to take to the new land and left behind what God asked Abram to leave behind. We too follow by giving all Jesus asks us to give Him and leaving what Jesus asks us to leave. What was a baby Step of **Alertness** Abram took? He continually built altars to commune and worship his God. We must consistently stay close to Jesus so we will be alert to His leading. What was a baby Step of **Faithfulness** Abram took? We cannot say Abram was perfect, but we can say he is faithful as he continued to come back to the Lord and follow Him. We want our lives to be characterized by moving towards Jesus more and more as we leave the maze.

OUT OF THE MAZE WITH THE LORD

Just like Abram, there will be a day that each of us leaves the maze of life. That day may be sooner for some or later for others, but King David gives us an interesting view of the maze from God's vantage point, *"You (God) saw me before I was born. Every day of my life was recorded in your book. Every moment was laid out before a single day had passed"* (Psalm 139:16 NLT). As we live these days that are marked out for us, Proverbs 3:5–6 becomes very powerful and practical to be quoted, read, and lived in the throes of the maze.

Because of its familiarity, the significance of Proverbs 3:5–6 can easily be overlooked, but let us conclude our walk together in the maze by taking a fresh look at Proverbs 3:5–6 through the eyes of Abram.

Trust in the LORD with all your heart (Proverbs 3:5a)

Abram would tell us this is the Step of **Willingness**. Trust has the idea of putting the full weight of ourselves on something. We willingly put the weight of our decisions, relationships, careers, everything on the Lord. The Lord can handle anything and everything that we can put on Him.

and lean not on your own understanding; (Proverbs 3:5b)

Abram would tell us this is the Step of **Obedience**. We lean on the LORD by obeying His Word and not following our thoughts, ideas, or opinions. This is why it is important to get to know God and His Word, because in following Jesus this is how we trust Him.

in all your ways submit to him, (Proverbs 3:6a)

Abram would tell us this is the Step of **Wholeheartedness**. We place everything we have at the Lord's disposal and discretion. This is a way of giving ourselves to the LORD with all that we have.

and he will make your paths straight. (Proverbs 3:6b)

Abram would tell us this is the Step of **Alertness**. Be alert to the paths God wants you to take. The more sensitive we are to Jesus the clearer it becomes to us which paths He wants us to take.

Abram would tell us both Proverbs 3 verses 5 and 6 are the Step of **Faithfulness**. Together they paint a picture of God's faithfulness to us and challenge us to faithfulness in our own lives. When we are faithful to do the things God says, then we will be where God wants us to be, doing what God wants us to do; today, tomorrow, five years from now and when we finish navigating life's maze.

***Trust** in the Lord with all your heart
and **lean** not on your own understanding;
in all your ways **submit** to him,
and he will **make** your paths straight.*
Proverbs 3:5–6

MY BABY STEP

THE BABY STEP WITH BOB

➢ How does "Baby Steps" apply to following God's will in life's maze?

➢ How is Psalm 77:19 an encouragement to us as we look back on our time in the maze of life?

Your way went through the sea and Your path through the great waters, but Your footprints were unseen.
PSALM 77:19 (HCSB)

THE IMPORTANT STEP
WITH OURSELVES

➤ In a sentence or two, how would you summarize each of the five steps and **what they mean to you?**

- The Step of Willingness

- The Step of Obedience

- The Step of Wholeheartedness

- The Step of Alertness

- The Step of Faithfulness

➤ Why are the steps compared to a compass? How does that help you understand how to apply the principles?

THE LASTING STEP
WITH ABRAM

➢ In a sentence or two, **from Abram's life** in the maze what do you want to remember?

- Abram's Step of Willingness

- Abram's Step of Obedience

- Abram's Step of Wholeheartedness

- Abram's Step of Alertness

- Abram's Step of Faithfulness

➢ How are we blessed today because of Abram? How does that encourage you in the maze?

THE NEXT STEP WITH THE LORD

➢ Which of the five steps does the LORD want you to take right now in your life?

➢ What specifically will you do to accomplish what the LORD wants you to do?

➢ When will you do what the LORD wants you to do?

➢ Is there someone you can ask to help keep you accountable to do what the LORD wants?

➢ Take Proverbs 3:5–6 and rewrite it below as a prayer. Then pray that to the LORD as a way of wrapping up your time in the maze with our good friend Abram!

Trust *in the* LORD *with all your heart*
and **lean** *not on your own understanding;*
in all your ways **submit** *to him,*
and he will **make** *your paths straight.*
PROVERBS 3:5–6

ENDNOTES

INTRODUCTION: THE FIRST STEP

[1] http://justus.anglican.org/resources/bio/139.html accessed 2/8/19. A prayer attributed to Bishop Richard of Chichester on 3 April 1253.

[2] See Psalm 119:105.

[3] Hebrews 12:2

[4] John Maxwell, an expert on leadership development, provides this helpful insight.

[5] Genesis 15:6; Romans 4:22–24; James 2:23

[6] Hebrews 11:6, 11

[7] Charles R. Swindoll, Abraham (Carol Stream, IL: Tyndale House Publishers, Inc., 2014), 260.

CHAPTER 1: THE VOLUNTOLD STEP

[1] https://www.urbandictionary.com/define.php?term=voluntold; accessed 2/27/2019

[2] *BADEW: Baird's Attempt to Define Everyday Words*; The author's own thoughts and attempts to define words, especially as used in *Navigating Life's Maze*.

[3] For continuity's sake, he will be referred to as Abram, meaning "exalted father," throughout the book. Most of our discussion will occur prior to God changing his name to Abraham, meaning "father of a multitude" in Genesis 17:5.

[4] To find out more about this spiritual conflict, read Paul's detailed description in Romans 7:7–25.

[5] Bruce Waltke, *Genesis: A Commentary* (Grand Rapids, MI: Zondervan, 2001).

[6] Ibid., p.204.

[7] John MacArthur, Author and General Editor, *The MacArthur Study Bible* (Nashville, London, Vancouver, Melbourne: Word Bibles, 1997), 332. "The Euphrates, where Abraham's family had lived. It is clear here that God's calling of Abraham out to Himself was also a call out of idolatry, as He does others (cf. 1 Thess. 1:9)." An interesting side note about is that idols still were an influence in the family as we see them resurface with Rachel. Rachel stole the household gods from her father Laban, whose name means double-minded, who wanted them back (Genesis 31:19; 31:25–37).

[8] Richard S. Hess, *Israelite Religions* (Grand Rapids, MI: Baker Academic, 2007), 179.

[9] A.W. Tozer, *The Pursuit of God* (Camp Hill, PA: Christian Publications, Inc., 1982, 1993), 24.

[10] Ibid., p.26.

[11] https://quoteinvestigator.com/2017/09/22/bible/ (accessed 2/17/19). Most attribute this saying to Samuel Clemens (a.k.a. Mark Twain); however, there is some question about who originally made the statement.

[12] https://germanstories.vcu.edu/struwwel/kaspar_e.html (accessed 2/24/19) The Story of Augustus Who Would Not Have Any Soup by Heinrich Hoffmann

[13] J.A. Motyer, *The Message of Amos* (Leicester, England and Downers Grove, Il: Inter-Varsity Press, 1974), 187.

[14] Hebrews 12:1

[15] From Martin Burnham's funeral program and also included in the picture section of the book: Gracia Burnham with Dean Merrill, *In The Presence Of My Enemies* (Wheaton, IL: Tyndale House Publishers, Inc., 2003).

[16] Tozer, *The Pursuit of God*, 27.

[17] Ibid., 30.

CHAPTER 2: THE 4-LETTER WORD STEP

[1] *BADEW: Baird's Attempt to Define Everyday Words*; The author's own thoughts and attempts to define words, especially as used in *Navigating Life's Maze.*

[2] Ammer, Christine (1997). *The American Heritage Dictionary of Idioms.* New York: Houghton Mifflin Reference Books.

[3] John 14:15; 1 John 5:3

[4] John MacArthur, *The MacArthur New Testament Commentary Ephesians* (Chicago, IL: Moody Press), 358. [Emphasis added by the author.]

[5] Also quoted from Psalm 14:1–3 and Psalm 53:1–3 in the Old Testament

[6] Monessa has graciously given permission to use her story of God's grace in the maze

[7] Andy Stanley, *The Grace of God* (Nashville, TN: Thomas Nelson, 2010).

[8] John 21:20

[9] Dietrich Bonhoeffer, 1906–1945, was a German pastor, theologian, anti-Nazi dissident. He was hanged to death on April 9, 1945, at the Flossenburg concentration camp in Germany.

[10] Dietrich Bonhoeffer, *Life Together*

[11] 2 Corinthians 5:7

[12] John 14:15

CHAPTER 3: THE MARTYR'S STEP

[1] John Foxe, rewritten and updated by Harold J. Chadwick, *The New Foxe's Book of Martyrs* (North Brunswick, NJ: Bridge-Logos Publishers, 1977), 324–326.

[2] John MacArthur, *The MacArthur New Testament Commentary 2 Timothy* (Chicago, IL: Moody Press), 10.

[3] https://www.dictionary.com/browse/martyr accessed 3/16/19

[4] *BADEW: Baird's Attempt to Define Everyday Words*; The author's own thoughts and attempts to define words, especially as used in *Navigating Life's Maze*

[5] Gene Helsel, *I Will Live* (ZEKE's Music: ZEKE IV, 1994), Used by permission.

[6] Bruce Waltke, *Genesis: A Commentary* (Grand Rapids, MI: Zondervan, 2001), 207.

[7] Matthew 6:21

[8] Jim Burns and Greg McKinnon, *Fresh Idea Series: Illustrations Stories and Quotes to Hang Your Message on* (Gospel Light, 1997), 73–74.

[9] Ray C. Stedman, *Friend of God* (Grand Rapids, MI: Discovery House Publishers, 2010), 198.

[10] https://www.insight.org/docs/default-source/default-document-library/70-resolutions---jonathan-edwards.pdf 8/1/19

[11] The Creed of a Bold Jesus Follower; a number of sources site this creed, the origin is unknown; the author has been identified as possibly from Zimbabwe but that is unconfirmed.

CHAPTER 4: THE VIGILANT STEP

[1] https://www.dictionary.com/browse/vigilant accessed 4/7/19.

[2] *BADEW: Baird's Attempt to Define Everyday Words*; The author's own thoughts and attempts to define words, especially as used in *Navigating Life's Maze*.

[3] Charles R. Swindoll, *The Mystery of God's Will* (Nashville; Word Publishing 1999), 39.

[4] Also see Genesis 15:6

[5] Bruce Waltke, *Genesis: A Commentary* (Grand Rapids, MI: Zondervan, 2001), 207.

[6] Mark Batterson, *Chase the Lion* (Multnomah, 2016), 122.

[7] Philippians 4:19

[8] Henry T. Blackaby and Claude V. King, *Experiencing God* (Nashville, TN: Broadman & Holman Publishers, 1994), 113.

[9] Gary Mayes, *Now What* (Wheaton, IL: Crossroads 1995), 130.

[10] Wayne Grudem, *Systematic Theology* (Zondervan, 1994), 162.

[11] Charles C. Ryrie, *Basic Theology* (Chicago: Moody Press, 1986, 1999), 53.

[12] Waltke, *Genesis: A Commentary*, 234.

[13] Allen P. Ross, *Creation & Blessing* (Grand Rapids, MI: Baker Books, 1998), 401. (The author omitted the Hebrew text from the quote to make it easier to read.)

[14] Rich Mullins and Beaker, *Sometimes By Step* (Kid Brothers of St. Frank's Publishing ASCAP/Edward Grant, Inc. ASCAP, 1991).

CHAPTER 5: THE STICK-TO-ITIVENESS STEP

[1] Story of Hachiko https://en.wikipedia.org/wiki/Hachik%C5%8D

[2] https://www.merriam-webster.com/dictionary/stick-to-itiveness accessed 4/14/19

[3] *BADEW: Baird's Attempt to Define Everyday Words*; The author's own thoughts and attempts to define words, especially as used in *Navigating Life's Maze*.

[4] Stephen Covey, *The 7 Habits of Highly Effective People* (Free Press, 1989).

[5] Bruce Waltke, *Genesis: A Commentary* (Grand Rapids, MI: Zondervan, 2001).

[6] See Genesis 22:1–19 for the account of Abraham offering Isaac.

[7] See Genesis 23:17–20 for the account of Abraham's purchase of the cave of Machpelah and the field near Mamre.

[8] Quoting Paul Tournier, *Reflections* (New York: Harper & Row, 1976), 142 from Warren W. Wiersbe Be Patient (Colorado Springs, CO: Chariot Victor Publishing, 1991), 26.

[9] W.H. Griffith Thomas, *Genesis: A Devotional Commentary* (Grand Rapids, MI: Wm. B. Eerdmans Publishing Co., 1946).

[10] Wiersbe, *Be Patient*, 92.

[11] http://gaither.com/news/%E2%80%9Cgreat-thy-faithfulness%E2%80%9D-story-behind-hymn; Public Domain, accessed 4/13/19.

SUMMARY: THE BABY STEP

[1] Andy Stanley, *The Grace of God* (Nashville, TN: Thomas Nelson, 2010), 31–32

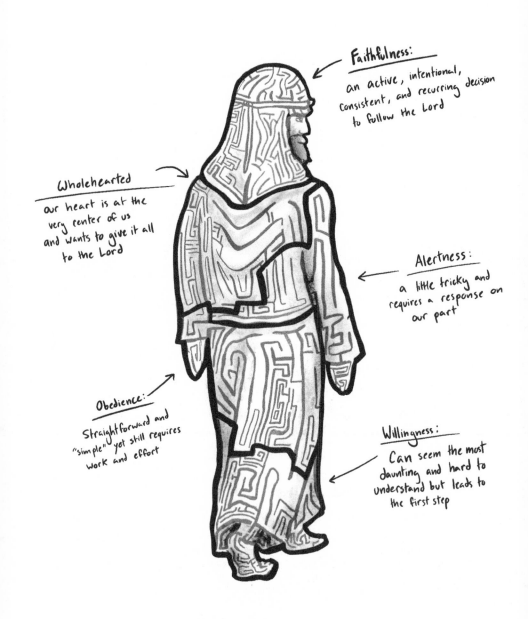

Faithfulness:
an active, intentional, consistent, and recurring decision to follow the Lord

Wholehearted
our heart is at the very center of us and wants to give it all to the Lord

Alertness:
a little tricky and requires a response on our part

Obedience:
Straightforward and "simple" yet still requires work and effort

Willingness:
Can seem the most daunting and hard to understand but leads to the first step

THE MAZE OF ABRAM DESCRIBED

ON THE OPPOSITE PAGE IS found the maze of Abram, which has been used throughout this book. Included with the drawing is a note to give the reasoning for the connection between that part of the overall maze and the specific principle of God's will. That particular portion of the maze has been used with the corresponding chapter.

APPENDIX B

THE TIMELINE OF ABRAHAM'S LIFE

GIVEN BELOW IS A SELECT timeline of Abraham's life that may be profitable during the reading and study of *Navigating Life's Maze*.

EVENT	SCRIPTURE	AGE
Abram born	Genesis 11:26	Abram's father Terah is 70 years old when he is born
Sarah	Genesis 17:17	Sarah is 10 years younger than Abram
God's promise that Abram will become a great nation	Genesis 12:1–4	Abram 75 years old

EVENT	SCRIPTURE	AGE
Abram leaves Haran	Genesis 12:1–4	Abram 75 years old
Abram marries Hagar	Genesis 16:3	Abram 85 years old; living for 10 years in Canaan
Ishmael is born	Genesis 16:16	Abram 86 years old
Promise of Isaac's birth in one year	Genesis 17:1–8; 21	Abram 99 years old
Abram's name changed to Abraham because he will be a father of many nations	Genesis 17:5–7	Abraham 99 years old
Abraham and his descendants circumcised	Genesis 17:9–14; 23–27	Abraham 99 years old

Ishmael 13 years old |

EVENT	SCRIPTURE	AGE
Sarai's name changed to Sarah because she will become the mother of nations	Genesis 17:15–16	Sarah 89 years old
Isaac is born	Genesis 17:17; 21:5–7	Abraham 100 years old Sarah 90 years old
Sarah dies	Genesis 23:1	Sarah 127 years old Abraham 137 years old
Isaac marries Rebekah	Genesis 24:67; 25:20	Isaac 40 years old Abraham 140 years old
Jacob and Esau born (Abraham's grandchildren)	Genesis 25:24–26	Isaac 60 years old Abraham 160 years old
Abraham dies	Genesis 25:7–8	Abraham 175 years old

THE FIVE W'S OF GOD'S WILL

THESE ARE FIVE PRINCIPLES THAT my Dad shared with me about pursuing God's will. I share these as another look at principles from God's Word in navigating life's maze to the will of God.

The Willingness of Heart

Father, if you are willing, please take this cup of suffering away from me. Yet I want your will to be done, not mine.

Luke 22:42 (NLT)

This is where we have a willingness to do whatever God wants us to do. God's will starts with the willingness of our hearts.

The Word of God

How can a young person stay on the path of purity?
    By living according to your word.
I seek you with all my heart;
    do not let me stray from your commands.
I have hidden your word in my heart
    that I might not sin against you.

Psalm 119:9–11

This is where we check to see what God's Word says specifically about God's will in our situation. Also, we want to examine the Word of God to see if it has any principles that we can apply to our situation. It is important to be obedient to God's Word.

The Wisdom of Counsel

Without counsel plans fail, but with many advisers they succeed.

Proverbs 15:22 (ESV)

This is where we listen to godly advice to help guide us to the will of God. Many times, the counsel of godly individuals shows us whether we are wholeheartedly committed to God or not.

The Witness of the Spirit

Do not be anxious about anything, but in
every situation, by prayer and petition,
with thanksgiving, present your requests to
God. And the peace of God, which transcends
all understanding, will guard your hearts and
your minds in Christ Jesus.

Philippians 4:6–7

This is where we sense the leading of the Holy Spirit in our lives.
We want to have a close relationship with Jesus Christ so we will have
spiritual alertness to what God is doing in our lives.

The Working of Circumstances

After I go through Macedonia, I will come to you—for
I will be going through Macedonia. Perhaps I will stay
with you for a while, or even spend the winter, so that
you can help me on my journey, wherever I go. For I
do not want to see you now and make only a passing
visit; I hope to spend some time with you, if the Lord
permits. But I will stay on at Ephesus until Pentecost,
because a great door for effective work has opened to
me, and there are many who oppose me.

1 Corinthians 16:5–9

This is where we examine our situations to see if God is using them
to help make His will known to us. The more we walk in faithfulness, the
more situations can be seen from God's perspective.

ACKNOWLEDGMENTS
Thanks
to ...

My small group, who graciously went through the very, very rough manuscript of *Navigating Life's Maze*.

Josh Barry for the incredible Abram maze and drawings used throughout *Navigating Life's Maze*.

Kris Udd for the amazing maps specifically created for *Navigating Life's Maze*.

Sarah Buchan for her photo of my family on the author page and her photo of me on the back cover (sarahbuchanphotography.com).

Suzanne Williams, my sister, for her keen eye, her astute observations, and her meticulous work in the editing process.

Jenny Wildman, who never ceases to read what I write and continually offers encouragement.

Noah for reading the manuscript and giving feedback.

Josiah for encouraging me to write and build the ministry.

Micah for letting me make him read my writings.

Lisa, my wife, for navigating life's maze with me for over 30 years; especially for going with me when I sensed God's direction for our lives, even though we didn't know what we were getting ourselves into.

ABOUT THE AUTHOR

Steve Baird

STEVE BAIRD IS A SPEAKER, writer, and founder of e710 ministries. He is a creative speaker and has been used by God to teach and preach God's unchangeable truths in America and around the world. He authored *Overcoming Life's Challenges*, the insightful book on dealing with trials from James 1:1–12. He founded e710 ministries based on the description of Ezra found in Ezra 7:10 (ESV), "For Ezra had set his heart to study the Law of the LORD, and to do it and to teach his statutes and rules in Israel." E710 ministries exist to assist individuals in encountering the written and living Christ, resulting in life change.

Steve is married to Lisa. They have been navigating life's maze together for over thirty years as Steve has been a youth pastor, senior pastor, college instructor, college administrator, Bible teacher, guest speaker, and author. Steve and Lisa have three young adult children: Noah, Josiah, and Micah. They are proud of each of their God-given uniqueness and what God is doing in their lives.

If you would like to find out more about Steve's writings, talks, or videos; if you would like to have him speak at an event, or if you would simply like to make contact with him, you can do so at e710ministries@gmail.com.

Overcoming Life's Challenges

AT THIS VERY MOMENT, EACH of us finds ourselves going into, in the middle of, or coming out of one of life's challenges. Whether the challenge is mental, emotional, relational, physical, or spiritual, we experience the testing of our faith daily. God's desire for us is not to merely pass

the test but to demonstrate our faith is genuine and develop the character of Jesus Christ. As we attend the school of hard knocks together, let us learn principles from the book of James that will enable us to Overcome Life's Challenges!

Overcoming Life's Challenges: Do I need to Know This for the Final? can be read by itself or along with the eight session *Overcoming Life's Challenges Participant's Guide* and video series.

"I have greatly enjoyed working through Steve Baird's *Overcoming Life's Challenges* with my men's small group. We found the book to be insightful and helpful in guiding our examination of the scriptural basis for the trials in our lives. I heartily recommend this book both for personal study and for small group use"

Kelly Walter
Founding Pastor | Rock Brook Church

Made in the USA
Coppell, TX
18 March 2021